An Observer's Guide to the

Killer Whales of Prince William Sound, Alaska

By Craig O.Matkin

Prince William Sound Books: Valdez, Alaska 99686.

Permission was generously granted by Camden House, Ontario, Canada to reprint the illustrations by K. Nagahama from *Orca, a Whale called Killer* by E. Hoyt. 1981.

Cover photo: Craig Matkin
ISBN 1-877900-03-6

Table of Contents:

Acknowledgments:

In a long-term study such as this, the list of contributors becomes nearly endless. In addition to those mentioned in the text, there have been many who have provided field assistance. Those contributors include Robyn Angliss, Kelly Balcomb, Karl Becker, Ralph Blancato, Peggy Bill, Guido Casciano, Laurie Daniel, Cathy D'Agrossa, Angus Ellis, Kirsten Englund, Molly Freeman, Matt Hare, David Grimes, Beth Goodwin, Lars Holtan, Mary James, Laurie Larsen, John Lyle, Lisa Madden, Dena Matkin, Elizabeth Miller, Nancy Murphy, Riki Ott, Laura Patty, Christina Schneider, Sue Ann Sikema, Ellen Weintraub, Ted West and Kate Wynn.

As a member of NGOS, Rick Steiner has provided invaluable field assistance and advice over the years and insight into the problem of killer whale interactions with fisheries. Bush pilot Jim Bishop demonstrated his unique flying and whale spotting abilities during several years of the study. Pilot Steve Rainy's unmatched eyes have repeatedly led us to the carcasses of beached whales. The late Pete Isleib provided generous logistic support and ideas in the early days of our work. Pete's undauntable spirit demonstrated that where there is a will there is a way. Marilyn Dahlheim supervised contract work for the National Marine Mammal Laboratory. Stephen Leatherwood supervised work completed under contract to Hubbs Seaworld Research Institute. Rich Corcoran, Harold Kalve, Mike Poole, Bill Lawton, Dave Janka, Rand Little, Dean Rand, Mark Sommerville, Wendell Jones and others went out of their way to lend assistance in keeping the operation going and locating whales in the field.

Various individuals at Chenega Village helped with logistics over the years. I thank my fishing crews on the F.V. *Lucky Star* for their patience and effort; in addition to their commercial fishing responsibilities, they worked overtime to supply field camps and identify whales.Jeff Poole and the tendermen of Seward Fisheries (Icicle Seafoods) provided invaluable logistic assistance over the years.

Cinematographers, Joel Bennett and Louisa Stroughton, were excellent field companions as were British filmmakers, Paul Reddish and Mike Potts, and Homer filmmaker, Daniel Zatz. Australian Broadcasting Corporation filmmakers, David and Liz Parer-Cook, provided film insight into the activities of the whales underwater. Elwood Miles of Miles Photo Lab in Nanaimo, B.C. has developed and printed our photographs with impeccable precision.

In addition, dozens of fishermen, tour boat guides, recreational boaters, and personnel at the several fish hatcheries operated by the Prince William Sound Aquaculture Association supported our work. Finally, we would like to thank all of those boaters who have contacted us over the VHF radio to report whale sightings.

Preface:

During the early 1970s, the study of whales was not as commonplace as it is today. However, at this time, several outstanding scientists began to stimulate scientific and popular interest in whales and dolphins. I owe my own early interest in whales to one of the true pioneers in whale and dolphin research, my professor of natural history at the University of California, Dr. Kenneth Norris. Dr. Norris possesses an incredible ability to observe and interpret natural events and, more significantly, to convey his excitement to his students. A second important influence was Dr. Francis Fay, my major professor at the University of Alaska, who guided my investigations of marine mammal-fishery interactions. Perhaps, the greatest inspiration for the founding of the North Gulf Oceanic Society (NGOS), however, was the late Dr. Michael Bigg. Dr. Bigg's pioneering studies in killer whale population biology have motivated dozens of killer whale projects worldwide including our own. His selfless dedication to his often unsupported research pursued in his free time serves as an inspiration to the rest of us. He has taught us that when there is a will to know, there is a way to find out.

The North Gulf Oceanic Society began in the late 1970s as an umbrella organization for a handful of Cordova based researchers to facilitate the writing of biological research proposals. Under the leadership of ornithologist, Pete Isleib, the group submitted proposals for the local study of birds, Stellar sea lions, harbor seals and whales. However, killer and humpback whales soon became the major focus of the group. Nancy Murphy and Dena Matkin led students from the *School for Field Studies* in a bluff-top marine mammal observation program in 1978. We had no boats; students observed whales from atop a high rock bluff at the South end of Squire Island near the present NGOS field camp.

In 1979, I obtained a small contract from the U.S. Fish and Wildlife Service to conduct a marine mammal censuses by running transects with my small fishing boat. Unfortunately, at that time I had not discovered the value of photoidentification as a census tool. However, as early as 1980, Olga von Ziegesar and Beth Goodwin, operating out of a small inflatable and camping on the beach, established the first humpback whale photoidentification program in the Sound identifying many of the humpback whales we still follow today. Although I had casually photographed killer whales as early as 1977, it was not until 1983 that Olga and Beth used my gillnet boat, *Kestrel*, to start a systematic killer whale identification program. NGOS, now a federally recognized non-profit marine research and education organization, received important funding that year from the Alaska Council for Science and Technology.

In 1984, Hubbs Seaworld Research Institute provided support to NGOS that allowed us a five month field season. That year we were able to clarify the membership of many of the resident pods with Graeme Ellis's first photographic catalog of the Sound's killer whale pods and Kirsten Englund's first recordings of the Sound's killer whale dialects. Olga and I were also able to put together the first humpback whale photographic catalog. Since 1984, however, our small but dedicated group has experienced constant difficulties in locating the funding to continue our research.

In 1985, Steve Zimmerman at the National Marine Fisheries Service in Juneau contracted us to survey blackcod fishermen experiencing killer whale depredations. Meanwhile, Linda Jones of the National Marine Mammal Laboratory supported humpback whale photoidentification. In 1986, the National Marine Mammal Laboratory in Seattle provided NGOS with the initial funding to examine conflicts between blackcod fishermen and killer whales in the Sound. In 1986, the State of Alaska's Marine Advisory program supported our killer whale photoidentification program and loaned us Rick Steiner to test techniques to deter killer whales from stealing fish from fishermen's longlines. The Sea Grant Marine Advisory program concerned with the role of killer whales in marine ecosystems supported various aspects of our research including Eva Saulitis' pioneering work on transient killer whale vocalizations and behavior.

At the time of the *Exxon Valdez* oil spill in March 1989, the North Gulf Oceanic Society's whale studies were among the few baseline ecological studies of the Sound's marine resources which would allow an accurate assessment of spill related damages. The National Marine Mammal Laboratory, therefore, funded three more seasons of NGOS research (1989-1991) to assess effects of the spill on the Sound's marine mammal populations. Because of the efforts of our independent researchers, we were able to supply data that was essential in measuring the effects of the spill.

During those troubled times, wildlife film companies including the British Broadcasting Corporation and Survival Anglia Ltd. provided funding in exchange for filming our research. Similarly, private donors and foundations have often aided our efforts. Jennifer and Ted Stanley, the Sulzberger Foundation, Lothar von Ziegesar Foundation, John and Anne Zinser and numerous others have made tax deductible donations to NGOS, providing money essential for equipment and supplies.

Each season NGOS must raise operating money. Fuel, film, and maintenance are required. Often, money has been available only after the field season is well underway. To insure that the research continues, NGOS members have at times donated their own time, money and equipment. Over the years, NGOS has slowly acquired research vessels and the state of the art equipment necessary for carrying out long-term studies. The boats required for the work are expensive and difficult to maintain under the challenging conditions of Alaska.

From the beginning, the North Gulf Oceanic Society has been a team effort on the part of stubborn, dedicated individuals pursuing the path of discovery. Prerequisites for researchers include the ability to repair engines and to cope with a remote wilderness environment sixty miles or more by water from the nearest town. Each individual has developed his or her own special area of study while contributing to the basic goal of identifying and enumerating individual whales and pods. This intimate, long-term knowledge of individual whales, their habits and health is essential to the preservation of the unique ecosystem of Prince William Sound which is being increasingly threatened by logging, oil transportation, fisheries interactions, tourism and other developments.

The NGOS Team - Key Players:

Olga von Ziegesar: Although my wife Olga's primary work is with humpback whales, she has been an integral part of the killer whale photoidentification programs since 1983. In 1984, during the Hubbs Seaworld project, she filled in for me while I was commercial fishing. Since then, she has provided invaluable assistance dividing her time between humpback and killer whale research, and maintenance and operation of her own small research vessel and raising our children.

Eva Saulitis: Eva recently completed her M.S. degree at the University of Alaska and specializes in the study of the vocalizations and behavior of transient killer whales. Her trained ear is proving invaluable in the analysis of killer whale vocal dialects. Eva and her field assistants have spent a number of long field seasons working from a small boat and living for months in a rain-drenched field camp. Eva has been the backbone of our field effort since 1988, spending more time in field than anyone else.

Lance Barrett-Lennard and Kathy Heise: Husband and wife, Lance and Kathy are master field researchers who have worked both in Alaska and British Columbia; they are as at home on a small boat as the whales are in their aquatic realm. Extremely dedicated, they seldom touch land during the peak of the research season. Kathy, who has a discriminating eye and excellent organizational abilities, assembled the most recent killer whale catalog (an NGOS publication). Lance specializes in acoustics and more recently in genetics. His doctoral research at the University of British Columbia is dedicated to unraveling the complex genetic relationships among killer whales in the North Pacific.

Graeme Ellis: Graeme has studied killer whales for over twenty years. As a teenager, he participated in the early capture and training of killer whales. This experience led to his eventual opposition to live captures. Graeme has an instinctive and uncanny understanding of killer whale behavior based on years of observations. In conjunction with Dr. Michael Bigg, he helped develop the photoidentification study of whales. By merely examining photos of their dorsal fins, Graeme can identify on sight hundreds of killer whales from populations ranging from California to Prince William Sound. Graeme works for the Department of Fisheries and Oceans, Pacific Biological Station, Nanaimo, British Columbia.

Dr. John Ford: John is the guru of killer whale acoustics. His pioneering work on killer whale dialects has won him world-wide acclaim. John's long hours spent locked in the lab analyzing whale calls has provided an incredible foundation for others to build on. John, Eva Saulitis, and members of the Vancouver B.C. Aquarium Laboratory are presently piecing together the detailed acoustic picture for the killer whales of Prince William Sound.

Chapter 1: Introduction

I first encountered the world of killer whales in 1976 while working for the Alaska Department of Fish and Game at remote Eshamy Lagoon in western Prince William Sound. The cruise across the Sound to Eshamy on the research vessel, *Montague*, took us past secretive and solitary minke whales, rambunctious groups of Steller sea lions, and finally into a large group of milling killer whales. The calm water and forceful exhalations of the whales created an enduring image of their serene power. I recall the five foot high, glistening dorsal fin of one male with an especially unique shape. The image of these first wild killer whales aroused my curiosity and created a lasting impression.

During that summer, I was stationed at a field camp at Eshamy Lagoon. My time off from working the salmon weir was occupied by watching for whales and reading the accounts of early studies of killer whales. Paul Spong's tales of kayaking with the killer whales in Johnstone Strait, Canada, fascinated me. The surreal images of kayaking alone in the fog surrounded by slow moving whales while playing languorous notes on his flute excited my imagination. Because of our ignorance of killer whale behavior at that time, his activities seemed extremely adventuresome, if not foolish. Many people feared approaching these awesome predators in a good sized boat, let alone in a kayak armed only with a flute! I also read of how Dr. Michael Bigg, Graeme Ellis, and Ian McAskie were learning to recognize individual killer whales in British Columbia using an innovative technique which Dr. Bigg called "photoidentification."

After the salmon were counted and scale samples taken for use in determining the age of the fish, kayaking the three mile length of narrow Eshamy Lagoon became my daily recreation. Because the narrow mouth of the lagoon often created a rushing tidal vortex, there seemed little chance of observing whales on these kayak trips. However, on one very calm and cloudy day, whale blows appeared suddenly off the mouth of the lagoon. Impossible, I thought! Pausing in the kayak, I listened as sharp exhalations became more audible. Now, dorsal fins were unmistakable. It appeared I would soon be kayaking with killer whales. How would these whales react to my presence? Perhaps, these Alaskan whales were different and more hostile than Spong's whales in Canada.

There was little time to ponder the possibilities for suddenly, three killer whales, two with tall dorsal fins, were abreast of the kayak and less than two hundred feet away. They were porpoising at high speed toward the shallow head of the lagoon. The wake of their passing rocked my small kayak. One of the three was not a killer whale at all but an all black false killer whale (*Psuedorca crassidens*) that we had seen outside the lagoon several days before. This rare sighting of a false killer whale in the Sound still stands as the northernmost sighting of this species.

My first thought was that the two killer whales were driving the false killer whale into the lagoon to kill and eat it. Each of the trio leaped clear of the water once, then twice, then a third time. Witnessing the towering splashes of each whale's reentry, I could feel the uncontrolled thumping of my heart. Intent on the spectacle, I failed to notice the other seven whales that had slid up behind me. I jumped in my seat as a loud exhalation nearby caught my attention. Paddle frozen in hand, I watched as the whales drew alongside and began to circle. However, eye contact with one of the whales soon eased my nervousness. These whales seemed aware, curious, and non-aggressive. This peaceful interlude ended abruptly when the two male killer whales and false killer whale returned at high speed. The kayak was between them and the other whales. Still thinking the killer whales were about to eat the false killer whale, I backpaddled to avoid being caught in the middle of the upcoming bloodbath. Surprisingly, they all met and circled peacefully near the kayak. The false killer whale acted as if it were just an all black member of the group.

The kayak drifted near the slowing whales. Now, they formed a tight group, diving synchronously with increasingly long periods between surfacings. Although the whales moved a few hundred feet during each dive, they reversed direction on each surfacing so that they stayed in the same area. Gradually, they became increasingly slow and quiet at the surface — a behavior we later came to recognize as "group resting." I drifted among the whales and waited as they dove. What was the explanation for what I had seen? I had my first introduction to the depth and complexity of killer whale behavior. Only years later would I realize just how unusual and mysterious was this first glimpse of killer whale life.

That evening questions ran through my head. Essentially, nothing was known about the lives of the killer whales in Prince William Sound. Could individuals be identified as in British Columbia? How many killer whales were there in the Sound? What was their social organization? Did they remain in the Sound or only pass through occasionally? As the light faded and their blows became shapeless sounds in the evening darkness, I made a commitment to study these whales. I had little idea of the years and time consuming effort it would take before resources could be mustered to mount a serious study — and how these studies would change my life.

Chapter 2:
Killer Whales in Prince William Sound

No other whale in the Sound carries such a forceful presence as the highly gregarious and often vocal killer whale. Occupying the apex of the food chain, these whales symbolize the raw productivity of the Sound's marine environment. Like our species, they depend on a healthy ecosystem. For them, the web of life begins with such seemingly insignificant creatures as the minute phytoplankton. In reality, it is upon these same phytoplankton that all who live in the Sound ultimately depend, from the largest whales to Steller sea lions, and to eagles, and to humans and bears feeding on salmon.

Killer whales can be found in all the world's oceans from equatorial waters to the northern and southern ice edges. They are most abundant in the colder, fertile waters of the North Pacific, North Atlantic and Antarctic. Their abundance in the North Pacific, including Prince William Sound, may be due to the large salmon and herring populations supported by the cold, nutrient rich upwellings common to these waters.

The largest member of the dolphin family, killer whales sometimes travel in groups of a hundred or more animals; but pods of five to thirty-five whales are much more common. When a large, dispersed group is traveling, whales may appear to stretch across the entire horizon.

Examination of the stomachs of animals taken when commercial whale hunting was still common revealed that killer whales eat everything from a variety of fishes, squids, and octopus to other marine mammals such as large whales, seals and

Fig-2. In the early days, most of NGOS's photographic work was done from an inflatable raft. One person steered while the other took photos. Note the shoulder brace supporting the camera to help obtain sharp pictures. Photo by Craig Matkin.

porpoises, and even occasionally birds (see Appendix 1). Different populations of killer whales may have distinct diets. For example, two populations occur in Prince William Sound: one eats primarily marine mammals, the other fish.

Because of their similar, vivid, black and white markings, rapid surface movements and explosive spouting, the Sound's Dall's porpoises are sometimes mistaken for killer whales. However, the sheer size of the killer whale (seven feet at birth to as much as thirty feet in mature males) easily differentiates them from the smaller Dall's porpoise. The killer whale's white markings also serve to distinguish it from all other whales.

The difference in size and weight of adult male and female killer whales is striking. Weighing up to eight tons, males grow several feet longer and several thousand pounds heavier than females. Males appear broader in the region of the foreflippers and narrower above the flukes and below the navel than females. While the female's dorsal fin is fulcate (sickle-shaped) even in maturity, a mature male's dorsal fin ceases to be fulcate and becomes elongated. It may reach five and a half feet in height. Likewise, at maturity, the adult male flukes become permanently curved downward at the tips. An adult male's foreflippers are nearly twice the size of the female's and look like broad, rounded paddles.

The life history of these whales reveals some striking similarities to humans — a top predator in the terrestrial food chain. The two species have comparable life-spans and reach sexual maturity at roughly the same age. Resident killer whales occur in pods which are not unlike the extended family groups of humans. Despite these similarities, the marine environment has shaped adaptations in the killer whale which have no counterpart in earthbound predators. Many of these distinctions are a result of the unique physical

Fig-3. Female killer whales have a sickle-shaped fin that does not change shape with maturity. Note the distinguishing notches on AB 14's fin and the "open" saddle patch — the black area inside the saddle patch. Distinctive markings like these make photoidentification a powerful tool for scientists. Photo by Eva Saulitis.

Fig-4. AB11 was first photographed in 1984. Note the fulcate dorsal fin indicating either a female or immature male. Photo by Craig Matkin.

Fig-5. By 1991, AB11's dorsal fin has straightened and grown into the distinctive dorsal fin of a mature male. Photo by Craig Matkin.

Fig-6. The large foreflippers of the adult male killer whale may help to cradle the female during breeding. Photo by Craig Matkin.

Fig-7. The downcurved flukes, which are permanently fixed in this position, distinguish the adult male. Photo by Craig Matkin.

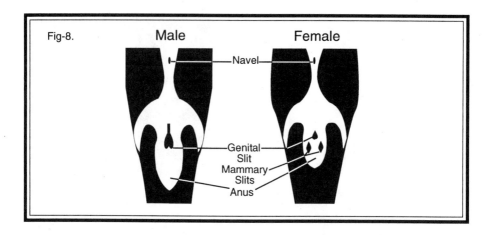

Fig-8. Male Female
Navel
Genital Slit
Mammary Slits
Anus

properties of the water through which the whales move.

Sound travels much faster in water than air, while light is rapidly absorbed as it penetrates the ocean's depths so that vision becomes very limited at depths greater than one hundred and fifty feet (considerably less during plankton blooms). Killer whales have, therefore, become dependent on listening and echolocation in finding their food. Vision, however, remains important at close range and at or near the surface.

The maximum size of terrestrial mammals is severely restricted by the effects of gravity, while the buoyant marine environment supports the world's largest creatures. A large body mass is advantageous for conservation of heat in these warm-blooded mammals. A layer of insulating blubber of two inches or more in thickness further protects the whale from its frigid environment. More important, the whale's blubber represents stored energy. While major prey, such as salmon and herring, are abundant during the summer feeding season, they are usually absent from inshore waters during the winter. Rich summer feeding means a thick blubber layer which can sustain a whale during a lean winter.

While we take the continuous availability of air for granted, the killer whale must function over ninety percent of the time while holding its breath. The killer whale can survive without breathing for longer periods than terrestrial predators because of adaptations in the circulatory system and an increased ability to store oxygen in the blood and body tissues. These adaptations increase the whale's ability to scour the water column in search of prey. Although capable of repeated dives to depths of five hundred feet or more, the killer whale is not considered a deep diver when compared to some other marine mammals such as the elephant seal which can dive to depths of over three thousand feet. The killer

Fig-9. A female killer whale breaches showing her genital and mammary slits. C. Matkin.

Fig-10. A male killer whale breaches showing his genital slit. Photo by Craig Matkin.

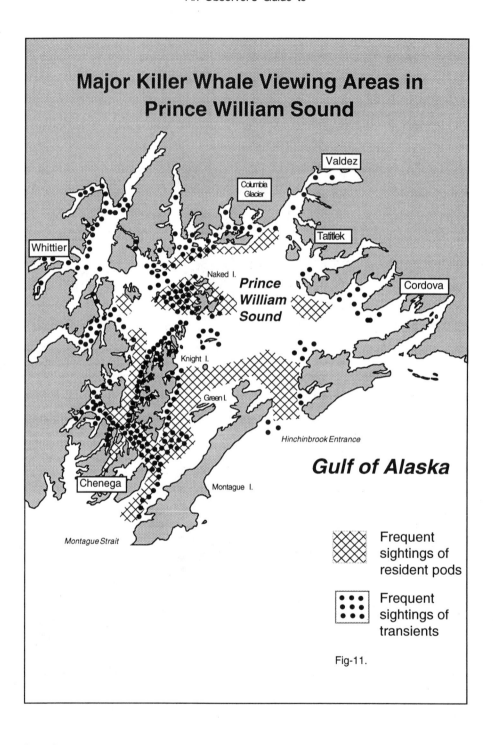

Major Killer Whale Viewing Areas in Prince William Sound

Valdez

Columbia Glacier

Tatitlek

Whittier

Naked I. *Prince William Sound*

Cordova

Knight I.

Green I.

Hinchinbrook Entrance

Gulf of Alaska

Chenega

Montague I.

Montague Strait

Frequent sightings of resident pods

Frequent sightings of transients

Fig-11.

whale may remain submerged for ten minutes or longer in rare instances; however, this pales in comparison with dives of over one and a half hours for the sperm whale.

Distribution in the Sound

There is probably no part of Prince William Sound that killer whales do not visit. We have seen whales or heard reports of their being observed in nearly every nook and cranny along the Sound's convoluted shoreline and near its several small communities. In fact, killer whales often appear at unexpected times and places. Researchers Kathy Heise and Eva Saulitis were once loading fuel from a beach in Gibbon Anchorage on Green Island when Kathy remarked to Eva, "We never see killer whales in here." Not two hours later, as they pumped the last of the fuel into the boat, the large dorsal fin of a male killer whale cleanly split the surface of the water no more than one hundred feet from where they stood. It passed in a shallow channel less than eighty yards wide.

Large groups of killer whales (10 to 100 or more) use the broad open passages and ocean entrances. Hinchinbrook Entrance, Montague Strait, and lower Knight Island Passage are good locations for finding killer whales, particularly in late summer and fall when pods aggregate and may remain in these areas for days. However, the open waters of the Entrance and the Strait can frequently be rough and rolly. The waters around Naked and Storey islands and west to Lone Island also produce many killer whale sightings, especially when the herring move up from the depths in the spring. Killer whales are also seen hunting Dall's porpoise in these areas. Killer whales are sighted in spring and during the height of the summer salmon runs in the northern Sound. Some killer whales spend considerable time scouring shorelines in pursuit of seals. These small groups of killer whales may suddenly show up in any of the myriad of restricted bays and coves around the Sound. Many of these sightings come from Herring Bay and other nearshore waters of Knight Island, from the shorelines and islands of the northwestern Sound, and from in front of glaciers where harbor seals rest on the ice floes. In these areas, the whales are often in small groups (5 or less) and are much less obvious than the larger groups that swim in mid-passage. They may be a startling surprise to a boat anchored in a quiet bay.

Over the past ten years most of our encounters with resident killer whales during the summer and fall have been in southwestern Prince William Sound. In the summer of 1989, we had three camps, one in the eastern Sound (Hinchinbrook Island), one in the southwestern Sound (Squire Island), and one in the northwestern Sound (Perry Island and Point Nowell). The results of our sightings and efforts from that year made it clear that the greatest rate of encounters with killer whales was in the southwestern Sound. The same killer whales photographed in the east and northwest were also recorded in the southwest; however, some whales were only photographed in the southwest. The narrower passages and calmer waters of the southwest Sound are more suitable for whale watching. This may also contribute to the higher rate of success in finding killer whales in that area. Likewise, killer whales and their major prey, salmon, tend to enter and exit the Sound through the southwestern passages.

Methods of study

One sunny, calm morning in 1977, I accompanied federal researchers following three humpback whales south of Chenega Island in southwestern Prince William Sound. This federally funded and permitted study was designed to follow the movements of humpback whales and Dall's porpoises by tagging them with brightly colored "streamer tags" visible at a distance. A metal flange holding the tag was shot into the whale from close range with a crossbow. This was before we realized that natural markings on humpback whales and even on Dall's porpoise made them easy to reidentify without tags. On this occasion the whales were uncooperative and stayed just out of range. It soon became necessary to force our presence on the whales, speeding toward them and attempting to tag into them when they surfaced. My discomfort increased with every tagging attempt. Was this technique really necessary? After hours of effort, it became obvious that this group of humpbacks could not to be tagged in this manner.

When the pursuit ended, the whales moved across the bay where they floated at the surface and rested. I had the urge to approach and examine these whales quietly. Nervously, I launched a kayak and paddled cautiously toward them. Would they allow me to drift alongside? Exhausted, they hung motionless at the surface; their breathing was rapid and labored. We had behaved no better than whalers pursuing their quarry to exhaustion. Quietly, in the kayak I was able to sit motionless within fifty feet of the resting whales. Their broad backs rose and arched slightly with each breath. After a while, it seemed that they were entering a deep sleep. Suddenly, a group of black and white Dall's porpoise shot in among the whales. Like bees, they buzzed around and under the humpbacks giving them no peace. As if our harassment were not enough, these playful porpoises joined the act. Reluctantly, the humpbacks high arched and began to dive. As the broad flukes of one whale slid up through the water, it was clear that they would break the surface directly beneath the kayak. I held my breath — the whale delicately moved its tail laterally and avoided the fragile craft. The humpback demonstrated much more consideration for me than we had for them.

After that day I decided that whenever possible, I would use non-intrusive techniques to study whales. Monitoring the effect of research activities on the whales and adjusting activities to cause the least disturbance possible became a primary consideration. Prior to the 1970s, most of our knowledge of whales came from data collected at whaling stations and on board whaling ships — data from dead or dying whales. New methods and new ideas for studying whales were just being developed. I resolved to commit my efforts to help develop and encourage these new, non-intrusive techniques.

The less intrusive a biologist can be when studying wild animals, the more likely it is that he or she will observe natural behaviors. Yet, often it is not possible to obtain the full story of the life of an animal without some method of marking or tagging individuals so they can be reidentified. Fortunately, both killer and humpback whales can be reliably reidentified by their natural markings. The first to realize killer whales were "naturally tagged" was Dr. Michael Bigg and his colleagues at the Pacific Biological Station in British Columbia. Each killer whale dorsal fin and white

Fig-12. The author records in his log photographs and scientific information which aid in the photoidentification and study of the killer whales. A telephoto lens supported by a shoulder brace mount and high speed black and white film helps the researcher capture razor-sharp pictures.

"saddle patch" behind the fin are uniquely nicked and marked. Similarly, the underside of each humpback whale's fluke displays a unique pattern. Both the color and series of bumps and ridges along the flukes' edge create an individual fingerprint. Pioneers such as Steve Katona, Hal Whitehead, and Chuck Jurasz first used these marks to reidentify individual humpback whales.

Graeme Ellis, a participant in the NGOS Prince William Sound killer whale project since 1984, contributes his expertise by identifying each killer whale in every frame of film we shoot each season. This insures that we are consistent in numbering and cataloging new whales each year and confirms or refutes our field observations. Not only does Graeme know the individual killer whales of Prince William Sound by heart, he also is familiar with every animal in Washington State, British Columbia and southeastern Alaska. He helps researchers up and down the Pacific coast match whales between areas. Observing a large group of killer whales with Graeme is like being guided through a cocktail party by a knowledgeable host. Individual dorsal fins are as familiar to him as human faces. Each whale brings a note of pleasant recognition like meeting an old acquaintance. He is quick to comment on the personalities and idiosyncrasies of individual whales. When not in the field among the whales, he can be found pouring over photographic negatives repeatedly examining each roll, frame by frame, until he has identified each individual. During this

painstaking process, Graeme is known to comment colorfully on the idiosyncrasies of whale photographers as well as whales! He is always pushing us to obtain "perfect" photographs with proper lighting, exposure, distance, orientation, etc. This is not always an easy task with Prince William Sound's rapidly changing weather and sea conditions.

Fig-13. The distinctive markings on the killer whale's dorsal fin and saddle patch make it possible to photographically identify and study individual whales. Note the general shape of Al1's (male, resident pod) dorsal fin, nick in the lower quarter of the aft edge, the shape of the white saddle patch, and the markings on the saddle patch. Photo by Craig Matkin.

Identification of individual whales is now the primary research tool used in all major killer whale studies — not only in the North Pacific but also in Norway, Iceland, the Crozet Islands in the South Atlantic, and off the Patagonia coast of Argentina. However, even for the trained observer, identifying each whale moving through open water is difficult. By freezing the action on high speed black and white film and later studying the negatives under a microscope we can pick out all the subtle, distinguishing marks and identify each individual.

Instead of the guns, traps, or snares used to sample and study some wildlife populations, the killer whale researcher is armed with lots of high speed black and white film, a telephoto lens, and an autofocus camera perched on a shoulder brace mount. With concentration and practice, the researcher can capture the razor sharp photographs needed for this work. Our goal is to identify every whale in each frame of exposed film. Some whales, however, are difficult to distinguish and require repeated photographs. Photoidentification allows us to keep track of each individual within a group or pod and to determine whether members are missing or dead. Bullet wounds and other marks are also quite visible in the photographs. Eventually, by analyzing the association of whales in the film over years of encounters, researchers can determine social relationships within a pod.

Approaching whales closely without disturbing them while obtaining good photographs requires experience, practice, and intuition. A whale's movements must be observed before attempting to get photographs. We fix our attention on a single whale or small group of whales and set a parallel course so that the whales are approached from the side

Fig-14. The right side of a killer whale is photographed just as the saddle patch is clearly exposed. AE10 (female, resident pod) has a more open saddle patch where the black intrudes into the white. Only residents seem to develop open saddle patches. Photo by Kathy Heise.

and behind. They sometimes react negatively to other approaches. Once a parallel course has been established, we edge in close only to take photographs and then slide away. By keeping note of the time the whales spend on the surface and submerged, our speed and course can be adjusted to synchronize our movement with theirs. After years of practice, one begins to intuitively anticipate the movements of the whales.

Because a killer whale moves quickly when it surfaces to breathe, the timing of photographs is critical. The whale is photographed just as the saddle patch is clearly exposed. Killer whales do not always follow a predictable course, especially when they are feeding. At these times, photography is nearly impossible; and long hours of waiting and watching are sometimes required. During these times, we collect recordings of their calls, retrieve fish scales or other evidence of feeding, observe behaviors, and attempt to determine the sex

Fig-15. Harassment is difficult to define. But when this male made this dramatic breach, we knew he was perturbed by our close approach for identification photographs. We quickly backed off. Photo by Craig Matkin.

of young whales. Invariably the rain starts, the sun sets, or a sudden wind picks up just as the whales' behavior changes to permit photography. Although various groups behave somewhat differently, most killer whale pods are often approachable and curious. When playing, socializing or traveling, they can be quite friendly and cooperative; however, when resting and feeding, they may often avoid approaches. At these times attempts to approach the whales may constitute harassment. Thus, familiarity with whale behavior is essential to avoid harassment.

"Harassment" is difficult to define precisely, but we look for signs that the whales are reacting to the approach of the boat. These situations are acknowledged and avoided. More subtle, long-term changes in the whales' activities due to harassment are difficult to detect or quantify. Definitely, a decline in numbers of whales in areas of increasing boat traffic may be a sign that the whales are being harassed. However, whales may also abandon an area for other reasons such as a diminished food supply. Because we cannot easily judge when whales are being harassed, both amateur and professional whale watchers should attempt to be conservative and cautious in approaching whales. Many whale watching boats in the Sound report that their most enjoyable experiences occur when they position themselves well ahead of the whales, shut down their engines, and allow the whales to decide for themselves how close to approach. Federal guidelines are being considered that would make any approach of a killer whale within one hundred yards (the length of a football field) illegal without a federal research permit.

Intrusive methods of observation may be justified only in the case of vital research. However, even within the scientific community, there is considerable debate concerning how much intrusiveness to allow and under what conditions. It seems ironic that an involved permit process and extremely rigid limits on activities are required of trained researchers taking identification photographs, while there is little regulation of the numerous commercial and recreational vessels operating around the whales. Dr. Bud Fay, a veteran walrus researcher, described the difficulties he experienced counting walruses on ice from the substantial distance specified in his permit only to watch a huge tanker plow through the floes and send the walruses fleeing into the water.

Chapter 3: Types of Killer Whales

"Resident" and "Transient" Killer Whales

If you were to meet Eva Saulitis speeding across the Sound in her tiny outboard driven boat or following a pod of killer whales, you might well wonder how such a young, soft spoken graduate student could survive in this remote and often hostile wilderness environment. Yet, Eva not only survives in this environment; she actually thrives here, for she senses that she is on the edge of a unique discovery — a discovery which will add to our understanding of killer whales.

Twenty years of photoidentification of killer whales has resulted in many surprising discoveries. No theory has created more of a stir than the notion that two distinct types of killer whales roam the same waters. One type, known as "residents," feed on fish. The other type, termed "transients," feed on marine mammals. In the Sound, Eva Saulitis picked up the early threads of evidence and found fascinating support for this concept. By laboriously searching out and patiently following the often reclusive transient whales of Prince William Sound, she was able to document their habits and found them to differ markedly from the resident whales. The problems presented by the remoteness of the area, unpredictable weather, and low budgets were half the battle in completing her work. The second half was her boat, dubbed the "Dorky Orky" that was donated to our project. With two tired outboards that were inclined to die at critical moments, this sixteen foot runabout gave Eva a good education in mechanics and survival on the water. We realized later that the foam core of this vessel was slowly absorbing water through minute pinholes in the outer skin. It was unsinkable, but it gradually got so heavy that the outboards could hardly move it. With tenacity and a more seaworthy vessel, Eva persevered. For months at a time, she has worked out of a small, damp, island tent camp, sixty miles from the nearest town. Tracking the elusive "transient" whales, she has documented their behavior and recorded their infrequent and unique vocalizations.

Occasionally, Eva observed killer whales involved in thrilling chases and kills. One morning, she watched five transients in pursuit of a small group of Dall's porpoises. The chase began at the surface and continued below. The whales followed one porpoise which tried desperately to outrun them. For a short distance the porpoise was faster, but it was not long before it tired. Ramming the hapless porpoise with their heads, the whales repeatedly sent it rocketing fifteen feet into the air as they followed behind (see Fig-43).

The terms "resident" and "transient" were first used by Dr. Michael Bigg as names for two distinct populations of killer whales he described in British Columbia. Residents could be reliably found in inside waters during the spring, summer, and fall. The transients were observed infrequently and sightings were long distances apart. The resident whales appeared in large groups that spent much of their time during the summer months eating salmon in the passages between Vancouver Island and the mainland. The transient whales, were found in small groups, slinking along the shorelines eating other marine mammals. Dr. Bigg's work concentrated on the social structure of the resident whales. Only recently have other workers such as Alexis Morton and Robin Baird in Canada and Eva Saulitis in Alaska spent the long hours necessary to unravel some of the details of the lives of transients.

When we first began our studies in Prince William Sound, it seemed to make little sense that two types of killer whales would exist in the same area and not interbreed or even associate with each other. No other mammalian species are known to have populations that share a common territory but do not interbreed. Why would the transients not eat the abundant fish they encountered? Why would the residents allow Dall's porpoise to swim along with them and not attack? With our naive eyes, we saw few differences between the groups of whales at first. However, after accumulating hundreds of hours of observations, our perceptions changed. Chugging along with the whales during encounters

Fig-16. Transient killer whales feed along the shoreline searching for harbor seals, sea lions and other marine mammals. Note the sea lions huddled together up on the rocks. Photo by Craig Matkin.

that sometimes lasted more than twenty-four hours, groups of ten to fifty or more whales were observed mixing and traveling together. These groups of whales with stable membership (pods) were often observed eating salmon. It gradually became apparent that other killer whales, traveling in groups of changeable membership, never mixed with these pods and were seldom seen pursuing salmon. Generally, these whales were found in groups numbering five or less, and the group membership was not always consistent. Since they often traveled quietly along shorelines, they were easy to overlook. These "other whales" were much more difficult to approach and photograph, which often left us frustrated with poor identification photographs. They were the only whales observed attacking other marine mammals.

Data began to indicate that as in British Columbia and Washington, resident and transient type whales also coexisted in Prince William Sound. However, closer observation seemed to delineate two or more stocks of transients. One spent most of its time in the Sound. This group of about twenty-one whales was called the AT1 group. The other transients are seen only occasionally, usually near the ocean entrances to the Sound and never in association with the AT1 whales. We call these whales the Gulf of Alaska transients, though we have no idea of their actual range or numbers. One of the mysteries of killer whale behavior is why the AT1 whales do not associate with the Gulf of Alaska

Fig-17. A rare photograph of resting transient whales from the AT1 group. Note the broad based, more triangular and pointed dorsal fins of these females. Photo by Eva Saulitis.

transients or with resident whales. On the contrary, resident whales from southeast Alaska and the Kodiak area seem to occasionally come to Prince William Sound and mix with local resident whales. Future genetic study of the DNA of these AT1 whales may provide clues as to their uniqueness.

Studies in other areas of the North Pacific now suggest complex webs of distinct killer whale societies that roam the contiguous waters of the North Pacific. The worldwide picture may include many types of killer whales that have yet to be described.

The development of specialized feeding habits may be the reason why resident and transient killer whales diverged. Although residents seem to be exclusively fish eaters while the transients eat primarily marine mammals, the ancestor to these forms may have fed on anything that was available. How would specialized feeding have evolved? In areas of seasonal salmon abundance some whales may have become more adept at feeding on salmon. Over generations the most successful salmon feeding whales proliferated. Eventually a separate culture of fish eaters may have emerged. Similarly, the most successful marine mammal eaters may have been precursors to today's transients.

Our observations of feeding resident whales reveal that they consume salmon and herring, but we suspect that they also feed on gray cod, flatfish such as halibut, and probably almost any other fish that are readily available (see Appendix 1) We have watched transients attack and consume Dall's and harbor porpoise and harbor seals. Steller sea lion remains have been found in the stomachs of stranded killer whales in the Sound. There have been reports of attacks on larger baleen whales; however, none of our group has observed such behavior. Apparently attacks on large whales in the Sound are rare occurrences.

Often, transient killer whales are seen traveling great distances, quietly patrolling the shorelines. Hardly noticeable, they slide along the rocky shores, traveling alone or in small groups, moving far back into bays and inlets. The element of surprise seems important in capturing harbor seals living along these shorelines. The capture of a seal is often sudden and sometimes marked by rapid vocalizations. Frequently, all that marks the site of the kill is an oily slick and shreds of skin and hair on the water's surface. Gulls may appear over the spot.

When in open water, transients sometimes exhibit erratic swimming behavior moving first in one direction then another, occasionally porpoising along at high speed. Such behavior usually indicates a chase. Kills of harbor porpoise and particularly Dall's porpoise usually occur in open water immediately following a chase. We have found inflated porpoise lungs with the head

Fig-18. Differences between Resident and Transient Killer Whales		
Characteristic	**Residents**	**Transients**
Size of Group	5 to 50+ (several pods may join)	1 to 7
Range	1000 miles+	500+
Habitat	Mid-passage, open water	Shorelines, protected bays
Travel	Headland to headland	Abrupt changes in direction
Dive times	3-4 short dives followed by a long 3-4 minute dive	Irregular dive times often greater than 5 minutes; some times as long as 15 minutes
Diet	Fish	Primarily marine mammals
Dorsal fin	Typically rounded tip, fulcate shape	More pointed, triangular

attached floating at the surface near transients, providing positive evidence of a kill. Interestingly, on rare occasion we have watched transients pursue fish.

Subtle differences in movements and behavior between these two types of killer whales become apparent after hours of observation. Alex Morton found that transients remain submerged an average of over six minutes while the average dive time for a resident whale is less than three minutes. My observations suggest transients also tend to arch their backs higher than the residents do when making a dive.

Resident whales forage down the middle of the broad passages between islands or between islands and the mainland where salmon tend to school. Churning the water, the resident pods make no secret of their location. When feeding, they are often spread out as singles or pairs across a distance of several miles or more, communicating through repeated social calls. The silent and secretive movements of the transients along shorelines contrast sharply with the behavior of the residents.

The social structure of residents and transients appears to be different. In resident pods, offspring travel near their mothers their entire lives. These maternal groups are composed of a mother and her offspring and are the building blocks of resident pods. Pods are defined as associations of maternal groups that travel together over fifty percent of the time. Transients, on the other hand, travel in groups that may exchange members. For example, while we always expect to see the same whales when we approach the resident AE pod, the transient whale AT1 may sometimes travel with AT12 and AT14 or with AT2 and AT3 or alone.

There has not been enough long term observation of transients to understand the social structure; hence, we refer to these aggregations only as "groups."

Often resident killer whales move in well defined pods that typically number between eight and forty whales, although they may join into "superpods," a grouping of several or more pods. These superpods may number over a hundred whales and sometimes seem to stretch to the horizon with the vapor from their blows scattered across the water in all directions. Aggregations of transients of this size have never been observed. Transient groups generally tend to number less than seven whales and often consist of groups of three or four whales. In all but one of the resident pods (AI pod, 6 whales) identified in the Sound, the membership exceeds eight whales. The current largest resident pod in the Sound, AJ pod, is composed of 31 whales. The seldom photographed AX pod (listed as 54 whales in our catalog) is thought to be more than one pod.

The experienced observer can distinguish differences in the body form and color patterns of residents and transients. The transients appear to have stockier bodies while their dorsal fins are broader at the base and more triangular and pointed than the narrower, more sickle-shaped fins of the residents. The dorsal fins of some transient whales, particularly those that only infrequently enter the Sound, are often replete with great gashes and nicks giving the impression of a more difficult existence, although the origin of these injuries is unknown. The white saddle patch below and behind the dorsal fin of transients tends to sweep farther forward to near the leading edge of the fin and appears to be larger than that of the residents (Figs 37-8). Only residents seem to develop "open" saddle patches where the black intrudes into the white area (see. Fig-14).

Initially, transient whales were thought to be almost always silent — perhaps a necessity when hunting marine mammal prey that could hear them. Eva Saulitis has found, however, that they sometimes make what she terms "quiet calls" when hunting — calls that are very difficult to pick up on hydrophones (underwater microphones). When they vocalize, their calls can be loud, sirenlike calls unlike any made by resident whales. Lone transients may repeat variations of these loud calls for hours at a time. Public radio commentator, Noah Adams, was fascinated by what he described as the repeated, mournful calls of the solitary transient whale. Transients produce the clicks used for echolocation only irregularly and generally only when they move along shorelines.

Resident whales use calls and call patterns unique to each pod. And, they use them nearly constantly. As Dr. John Ford discovered, each resident pod has its own "dialect" which distinguishes it from all other pods. An experienced listener can determine the identity of a pod just by listening to the calls. Unless they are resting, resident whales are nearly always vocalizing. Their calls are often accompanied by rapid echolocation clicks while ranging the passages in pursuit of fish. Researchers frequently locate resident whales by listening for their calls with a directional hydrophone. This apparatus is basically an under-water microphone attached to the center of a parabolic dish that is backed with soundproof neoprene. The dish is lowered into the water on a pole and rotated until the direction of the calls is isolated.

Resident killer whales inhabit Prince William Sound for at least a portion of the spring, summer, and fall. Observations from fishermen indicate that the major pods are in the area during much of the winter as well. Although they may range offshore at times, summer and winter sightings suggest they do not travel far. Unlike most humpback whales, killer whales make no seasonal migrations to warmer southern waters.

Home ranges for even the most familiar resident pods remain unknown. However, the extent of their movements has been partially determined by tracking the frequency and locations of encounters. Each pod may have its own unique home range. It is suspected that the resident pods encountered most frequently (the AB, AI, AN10, AN20, AE, AK, and AJ pods) are seldom, if ever, more than a few hundred miles from the Sound. Two resident pods that center their range in southeast Alaska (the AG and AF pods) have visited Prince William Sound on several occasions. These pods traveled a distance of over four hundred miles. Another resident pod, the AD pod, has been photographed over two hundred miles to the southwest of the

Fig-19. A rare sighting of the AG pod, whose normal range is in SE Alaska, in Prince William Sound. Photo by Eva Saulitis.

Sound in Kachemak Bay. Two pods, AD and AX, have been sighted over three hundred and fifty miles to the southwest in Kodiak Island waters, and we suspect these pods may center their range in that area.

Except for the AT1 group, transient whales are sighted much less frequently in the Sound than the residents and apparently spend most of their time outside the Sound. We suspect they travel great distances, because years may pass between sightings of a particular group; some groups have only been photographed once. The range of these whales is still a mystery, but they may move southwest along the outer Kenai Peninsula toward Kodiak Island and the Alaska Peninsula rather than toward Southeast Alaska. In Kodiak waters where there has been little photographic effort, only one photograph match has been made with a transient whale sighted in Prince William Sound. This same well marked transient whale, AT51, was also sighted twice in Kachemak Bay. Possibly, increased photographic effort in the Kodiak area would add substantially to our knowledge of the ranges of killer whales photographed in Prince William Sound. There have been no matches of transient whales between Southeast Alaska and Prince William Sound.

While the ranges of the Sound's transients remain unknown, photographs show that some transient whales in Southeast Alaska repeatedly travel as far south as Puget Sound over nine hundred miles away. Transients seem to travel regularly between British Columbia and Southeast Alaska and vice versa. Recently, a whale photographed in Southeast Alaska was sighted in Monterey Bay, California over fifteen hundred miles distant.

Contrary to our original expectations, over the last ten years in the Sound, resident whales have never been observed associating with transients. On one occasion, after watching a group of transient whales for several hours, Olga and I heard calls of resident whales growing louder on the hydrophone. Suddenly, the transients vanished, and the residents filled the area, saturating the undersea world with their calls. Eva Saulitis has watched residents pass in mid-channel while transients moved along the shoreline, both groups vocalizing yet maintaining their respective distances. Lance Barrett-Lennard and Kathy Heise watched a group of resident pods form a tight group in response to the approach of transients. The transients eventually turned, increased their swimming speed and left the area. The tight grouping of resident whales when transients are nearby has been recorded on several other occasions. Whether this reaction is a defensive maneuver is uncertain. Although mixing and socializing is common among the various resident pods, the transients remain aloof, apparently mixing only with other transients.

Most of our encounters with transients have been with the AT1 group. Until recently, these whales were sighted as frequently as some of the resident pods. They seem to center their range in Prince William Sound. Other transients that occasionally enter the Sound from the Gulf of Alaska are not well-known. On one rare occasion Eva watched three of these approach the site of a recent Dall's porpoise kill made by members of the AT1 group. The two groups never mingled but began traveling in the same direction, with the AT1 group about an eighth of a mile behind the other whales. After swimming the same course for about seven miles, each group turned and traveled in opposite directions. The relationship of the AT1 group with other transients is unknown, but future genetic studies may provide insight.

Distinct fish eating (resident) and marine mammal eating (transient) killer whales may not be unique to the North Pacific. Preliminary photoidentification studies of killer whales in Norway suggest that the same phenomenon exists there. In the Antarctic, Russian scientists studied hundreds of killer whale stomachs taken by whalers and distinguished two distinct types of whales, a fish eating type and marine mammal eating type. American killer whale researcher, Kenneth Balcomb, has made field observations that support the Russian research. He observed smaller killer whales, apparently yellowish from growth of microscopic diatoms on their skin, feeding on small fish and traveling in large schools along the Antarctic ice edge. These he distinguished from smaller groups of larger killer whales feeding on marine mammals while patrolling the offshore waters.

Feeding specialization in killer whales, however, is not necessarily universal. Scientists studying killer whales in Patagonia along the Argentina coast have discovered identifiable killer whales which shift their diets seasonally between fish and marine mammals. Certainly, killer whales have different habits and social structures in the various corners of the world's oceans. Recently, a new type of killer whale has been repeatedly photographed in the offshore waters of British Columbia and southeastern Alaska. These killer whales travel in large groups of changing composition, and do not appear to associate with the inshore resident and transient killer whales. It seems that a mosaic of killer whale cultures, perhaps no less diverse than those of *Homo sapiens*, may span the world's oceans and await our discovery.

Resident Pod Social Structure

When observing a pod of killer whales, one's eyes are automatically drawn to the imposing five foot dorsal fin of the mature males slicing through the water. Their large size and dramatic fin give the impression that the male killer whales must be the powerful leaders of the pack. Therefore, it was quite a shock to our male chauvinism when Dr. Bigg and his associates in British Columbia announced that resident killer whale social structure was centered around and possibly directed by the females. Jeff Jacobson's extensive observations of resident killer whales suggest that females are the instigators of pod activities. We also have watched females (sometimes accompanied by young calves) taking the lead when the whales were removing hooked blackcod from the lines of commercial fishermen.

This "matrifocal" society, centered around the females is a logical extension of the social structure of resident pods. The basic resident killer whale social unit is the maternal group, composed of a female and her offspring of both sexes. When daughters mature and bear young, they initiate their own maternal groups within the pod, but are often found in close proximity to their mothers. Large pods which are seen traveling together are usually composed of several maternal groups. Typically, the adult female is accompanied by recent calves or juvenile offspring and then by older sons and daughters. It is not unusual to see large males with towering dorsal fins following along behind their mothers. Offspring will remain with their mothers their entire lives.

This social organization is not completely unprecedented. Elephants and lions also have such matriarchal social systems, where females act as the head of the herd or pride. What is unique in resident killer whales is that neither male nor female offspring leave the maternal group. In all other well-known species, at least one sex or both sexes disperse when older to insure that breeding does not occur among close relatives. Although sperm whale groups are surprisingly stable, the adult males move between groups. Recently genetic studies indicate that pilot whales near the Faroe Islands have a social system similar to killer whales in which offspring of both sexes remain in the pod. These studies in pilot whales show that while an individual remains throughout its life in its birth pod, mating does not occur between pod members. Mating only occurs when several pods of pilot whales mix.

The resident killer whale's familial bonds are so strong that the only time a whale permanently leaves its pod and maternal group is when it dies. Likewise, never in twenty years of study in British Columbia and Washington nor in nine

Fig-20. The maternal group, composed of a female and her offspring of both sexes, is the basic social unit of resident pods. Here, matriarch AI 3 (second fin from the left) swims with her juvenile daughter (AI 4) alongside and her probable sons AI 2 and AI5 following behind. Photo by Kathy Heise.

years of records from Prince William Sound and Southeast Alaska has a member of one resident pod been observed to join another on a permanent basis.

Resident killer whales do not always travel in close formation, however. When feeding or traveling rapidly, the pod may be spread out over miles of ocean. During social sessions with other pods there may be temporary mixing between maternal groups. Mature males, perhaps spreading their genes, occasionally wander, showing up for short periods in pods other than their own. Genetic studies will eventually be the key to unraveling the mating system of killer whales.

When a pod is traveling slowly or resting, the whales generally arrange themselves in their maternal groupings. These tightly arranged groups in which individuals travel with their closest relatives facilitate our photoidentification efforts. Often, we will wait for these aggregations to form before taking pictures. Photography is most difficult when a pod or group of several pods spread out as individuals across a broad passage. However, often maternal groups will suddenly arrange themselves in pods like scattered soldiers scrambling into inspection lines. At these times, we have a narrow window of opportunity for photography. A peaceful afternoon of observing and recording scattered whales turns suddenly into a scramble to prepare cameras, films, light meters and other equipment as the whales line up.

Knowledge of each maternal group greatly aids in the identification of individual whales. Graeme Ellis may pour through tens of thousands of photographs a year identifying killer whales from California, British Columbia, and Alaska. Identification of a single whale signals to him that other members of the maternal group are likely to occupy adjacent frames. By examining the order in which whales appear on the film, he can form hypotheses as to relationships between individuals. This process is then assisted by statistical analysis. However, only genetic analysis will finally prove the hypotheses we have developed concerning relationships within pods.

It is doubtful that transient and resident whales share the same social structure. The concept of a pod as defined for residents does not seem to hold true when applied to transients. It is true that transients appear to travel in single maternal groups. However, unlike the resident whales, transient groups seem to occasionally change in membership, casting doubt on the idea that they are true maternal groups. Calves appear only infrequently. In fact, no calves have been observed between 1985 and 1993 in the AT1 group (21 whales total). As observations of transients accumulate, we will hopefully develop a better understanding of their social interactions and the structure of their groups.

Life History and Population Biology of Resident Killer Whales

Observations of resident killer whales made over the years in British Columbia and Alaska, coupled with observations of captive whales has created a fairly detailed picture of their life histories. Much of this information comes from the past twenty years of study of wild whales in British Columbia with support from the Prince William Sound studies. Transient killer whales may share similar life histories, but differences between the two types may yet await discovery.

At birth, killer whales are about seven feet long and weigh around four hundred pounds. From studies of captive whales, it appears that killer whales carry their young for about seventeen months before giving birth. In our area, most calves are born in winter which suggests the most active breeding period is in late summer and fall, a time when increased sexual activity is indeed observed. Calves may be conceived within the multi-pod social aggregations that occur at that time of year.

Young whales may nurse for a year or more; however, the average age at weaning is not known. We have observed nursing activities many times. Typically, the mother slows to a near stop, arches her back slightly and holds her flukes still. Her calf comes from below to tap its snout on her mammary slits (located about a quarter of the body length up from the flukes) and feeds on the discharged milk. The nursing episodes we have observed have lasted no more than a minute.

Killer whales are slow to mature. Generally, at about fifteen, females are mature and have their first calf. A female will produce from two to four calves in a lifetime with an interval of four to ten years between calves. When they reach forty, fertility seems to end. Usually by this time, the whale has become a grandmother.

Fig-21. This calf, AB37, was apparently the product of a difficult birth as indicated by the severe scaring along the sides and back of the tiny whale. Photo by Craig Matkin.

Males also become sexually mature around the age of fifteen. Because of the sudden growth of the dorsal fin at this age, these maturing males are nicknamed "sprouters." A small curved dorsal fin in a young male will straighten out and grow to a final height of up to five and half feet (see Figs-4 & 5). The growing dorsal fin often appears to wobble as if not yet fully strengthened by the rapidly growing connective tissue. As a male's dorsal fin grows, his foreflippers also grow longer and broader (see Fig-6), and his flukes begin to curve down at the tips (see Fig-7). By twenty-one years, the towering fin has fully developed and the whale is physically mature.

Mature male killer whales both in the wild and in captivity sometimes develop a collapsed dorsal fin. Although much speculated upon, the reasons for this collapse are still unknown. We do know, however, that shortly after the *Exxon Valdez* oil spill the dorsal fins of two whales, AB2 and AB3, began to curve down at the tips. Over the next two years we watched as the fins continued their downward movement and eventually lay down alongside the body. We suspect that this collapse may be a sign of stress or of ill health. In captivity the dorsal fins of male killer whales invariably collapse. In the case of at least two captive whales, dorsal fins have had to be amputated because of deterioration. In British Columbia a male killer whale was observed to have died shortly after his fin collapsed. However, in Prince William Sound, three males with collapsed fins (AB2, AB3, AN1) are all still alive as of 1993. Once a killer whale's fin begins to collapse, it never regains its original state.

Until it begins to grow, the dorsal fin of a male is indistinguishable from that of a female. For this reason, dorsal fin shape alone cannot be used to distinguish younger males from females. Unless a whale is accompanied by a calf (mature female) or has a large dorsal fin (mature male), the sex can only be determined with certainty by observing the location of the genital slit, presence or absence of mammary slits, and color pattern on the underside of the whale (see Figs-8, 9 & 10).

Because social bonds are so permanent, mortalities within resident pods are easily determined. A whale missing after repeated encounters with its pod over the course of a year can safely be presumed dead. Never has a missing whale returned to its pod after a prolonged absence nor has permanent migration of whales between resident pods been photographically documented. Our research confirms the surprisingly low reproductive rates and correspondingly low mortality rates observed for killer whales in other parts of the world. Since 1984, the average natural mortality rate for most Prince William Sound's resident killer whales has been an incredibly low — 1.5 percent per year. However, one pod, AB pod is excluded from this calculation. We have lost only nine whales in eight years from five pods that totaled eighty-seven whales in 1984. Some pods such as the AJ and AN10 and AN20 pods have average mortality rates of less than one percent per year. This means that for a pod of thirty whales (such as AJ pod), there is only one death every three or four years. The average recruitment rate (number of new calves counted each year) for these five pods is about 4.2 percent. This means that a pod of about thirty whales will produce an average of about one calf per year. Since 1984, most resident pods in the Sound have been growing. In fact, these five pods now contain one hundred and one individuals. It is not known why the pods are increasing in number.

Although mortality rates are low for whales over six months of age, we now suspect that about half of all newborn whales perish shortly after birth and before they are photographed and counted. Although the cause of this high rate of infant mortality is not known, stresses must be considerable during late winter when most killer whales are born. If the infants survive the first months of life, their chances for survival probably increase dramatically.

Although no killer whale has been followed from birth to old age, it is clear they are very long-lived. The life expectancy of killer whales is calculated from their mortality rates. The low death rates determined in Canadian studies indicated a average life expectancy of twenty-nine years for males and fifty years for females. Maximum ages were estimated fifty to sixty years for males and eighty to ninety

Fig-22. The author removes the stomach and intestines from a stranded whale. Trophy seekers had already removed the head. Photo by Olga von Ziegesar.

years for females. Short finned pilot whales have comparable maximum ages of sixty-three years for females and forty-six years for males.

These life expectancy figures are disputed by oceanaria where captive killer whales appear to die at much younger ages. However, a growing body of evidence from observations of wild whales tend to support the longer life expectancy figures. In British Columbia photographs were taken in 1965 of a mature female estimated to be a minimum of fifteen years old at the time the picture was taken. Current photographs (1992) are available of the same whale indicating that she is now at least forty-two years old. A male with an adult dorsal fin (males are about twenty years old when the dorsal fin is fully developed) photographed in 1972 in British Columbia is still alive today, indicating that it is at least forty-one years old.

Estimates of ages developed by counting growth rings in the teeth created some additional confusion regarding the ages of killer whales. Many species of mammals can be aged by counting the growth rings in their teeth. Layers are deposited in killer whale teeth; but after about twenty-five years of age, counting the annual rings have been judged unreliable. Recently, scientists using a new, but unproven, technique examined a slice of tooth from a killer whale stranded in Prince William Sound. They found sixty-six layers. Unfortunately, at the present time the value of annual layers in teeth as a means of determining the age of killer whales remains uncertain.

Teeth are a necessary tool for the survival of a killer whale. Each killer whale has about forty-four large, widely spaced, conical teeth. Gum disease and dental problems seem to be a major cause of death in older whales. They may also suffer from arteriosclerosis and vascular problems similar to humans. Since mature whales have no predators, it is likely that age and disease are the major factors causing death.

Chapter 4: Killer Whale Pods in the Sound

Our files contain over three hundred and twenty living whales sighted in Prince William Sound. Since 1984, when many of the Sound's killer whales were first thoroughly photographed, we have identified a total of at least eleven resident killer whale pods totaling some two hundred and fifty whales. However, this number changes constantly as whales are born and die, and occasionally when new pods are discovered. Some whales, photographed only once, have not been cataloged into pods. There are a few pods we encounter infrequently, and their exact composition and numbers have not been accurately determined. Total population estimates are further complicated because transient whales, unlike residents, do not maintain stable pods. We list them in groups, yet these groupings may change in number and composition. Transients sighted in the Sound total about fifty-two whales. However, many of these are seldom seen in the Sound. Some have been photographed only once. A core group of about one hundred and twenty-five resident whales in seven pods and twenty-one transient whales, tentatively considered the AT1 group, use the Sound regularly.

The well-known and frequently encountered pods of Prince William Sound are described below accompanied by photographs of easily identifiable individuals from each pod. A complete photocatalogue of Prince William Sound killer whales was published in 1992 and is available from NGOS. A standard

Fig-23. AB2. Two large adult males in the AB pod have completely collapsed fins — AB2 and AB3 (see Fig-57.). Photo by John Francine courtesy of Hubb-Sea World Research Institute.

Fig-24. The forward sloping fin is a distinctive characteristic of the male AB5. Photo by Lance Barrett-Lennard.

Fig-25. Two deep notches and the open saddle patch help to identify the female AB14. Photo by Eva Saulitis.

code is used to label pods, groups and individuals. The first letter in the code is A and designates the region, Alaska. It is followed by a second letter (A-Z) that indicates the pod. For example, AB3 is the third whale designated in AB pod. Each pod or group has a unique composition and personality.

AB POD

Encounters in the Sound with AB pod reach back many years. Originally, we dubbed this pod the "Bigg pod" after Dr. Bigg who motivated our original work. I photographed members of this pod (AB1, AB2, AB17, and AB24) as early as 1979. This has always been a friendly and curious pod. Even during our early encounters with AB pod, which numbered thirty-five animals in 1984, the whales were easy to approach. Often younger whales would charge up to swim in the propwash or beneath the research vessel.

The curiosity of some AB pod whales led them into conflict with the blackcod longline fishery. They were the first pod (and perhaps the only pod) to rob fishermen's longlines. Many suffered gunshot wounds in 1985 and 1986, and some of the wounded whales died. The pod contained 31 whales in 1986.

After the *Exxon Valdez* oil spill in March 1989, thirteen of the thirty-six whales that we counted in AB pod in 1988 perished either at the time of the spill or in the year following. From Puget Sound to Prince William Sound, no other known resident pod of comparable size has suffered so many mortalities in so short a time. Because many of the young whales in this group have died, there has been great concern for the future of the pod. In 1992-1993, the pod showed signs of slow recovery with three new calves born since 1991 and no additional mortalities. The pod numbered twenty-six whales in 1993 (see Fig-55).

Because of their playfulness, AB pod is a favorite of many people who travel through the Sound. Unfortunately, several of the most curious and friendly whales in the pod died at the time of the *Exxon Valdez* oil spill. The pod is easily distinguished by the collapsed dorsal fins of two adult males (AB2, AB3) and by the open saddle patches of some of the females. The fins began their collapse after the oil spill. The adult male with forward sloping fin, AB5, and female AB14 with two deep notches in her fin are other distinctive members of this pod. (AB11 as an juvenile male and adult is shown in Figs 4 & 5; AB 37 and her calf are depicted in Fig-21; AB32 and her calf, AB 47, see Fig-58.).

Fig-26. The AI pod is composed of a single maternal group. The matriarch, AI3, is second from the left. Her juvenile daughter, AI4, travels alongside while her mature sons AI2 and AI5 follow close behind. Photo by Kathy Heise.

Fig-27. AI1, a mature male, is distinguished by the nick in the lower quarter of the aft edge. Photo by Lance Barrett-Lennard.

Fig-28. AI2. Note the tiny nick in the upper third of the aft edge. Photo by Lance Barrett-Lennard.

AI POD

Photographed as early as 1982, AI pod numbered six whales in 1984 (including one new calf, AI4). As of 1993, the membership of the pod has not changed, although two males, AI5 and AI6, (possibly twins) have matured.

In the mid 1980s the pod traveled with AB pod a great majority of the time. It may be that this pod was in the final process of splitting with AB pod. The calls of AI pod are very similar to those of AB pod.

AI pod is composed of a single maternal group. The mother, AI3, and daughter, AI4, are the only females in the pod. Four tall graceful dorsal fins mark the remaining males, all believed to be sons of AI3. We frequently refer to this group as the "boys club;" it is rare to see four large males traveling so closely together. Maternal groups with several males often travel a short distance away from the rest of the pod. Perhaps, the large number of males in this group contributed to its splitting off to become a separate pod.

When alone, AI pod often travels in a tightly knit unit. The males AI1 and AI2 have distinctive nicks in their dorsal fins and are easy to identify. AI pod was present on several occasions when AB pod was raiding blackcod longlines, although no bullet wounds have been seen on these whales. Lately, AI pod has traveled more frequently with AE pod than AB pod. Continued study of this pod, its acoustics, and its relation to AB pod may provide a glimpse into one example of the mechanics of new pod formation.

AE POD

AE pod numbered thirteen whales in 1984 and currently (1993) contains fifteen whales. There have been four deaths and six births since 1984. The AEs were a very difficult group to approach and photograph in 1984. They seemed particularly shy of the boat, constantly turning away and spending long periods underwater. Graeme Ellis thought it might be my poor technique that prohibited the close approach. I thoroughly enjoyed his frustration after he also was rebuffed in attempts to get close enough for proper photographs. Because of their initial shyness and the lack of nicks and scars on some individuals, identifica-

Fig-29. AE1, a male, is easy to identify by his partially curled dorsal fin. Photo by Kathy Heise.

Fig-30. The female, AE10, has a very distinctive saddle patch. Photo by Kathy Heise.

tions of these whales were difficult in early encounters. Some AE pod whales were not clearly identified until 1985. Remarkably, they have become accustomed to the presence of researchers and now frequently approach and swim alongside the boat. Although AE pod is acoustically similar and probably closely related to AK pod, the two pods do not frequently travel together. AE pod is often seen swimming alone. One AE pod whale was photographed in 1977.

AE pod has been frequently sighted in May and June when other resident pods are not commonly encountered. They regularly travel in the northern Sound where tour boats observe them. They have a very distinct vocal dialect, and one large male with a curved dorsal fin, AE1, and the female, AE10, make the pod easy to distinguish.

AJ POD

AJ pod was first photographed in the Sound in 1977. This pod's presence has been somewhat sporadic; in some years it has only been photographed occasionally. Often, the pod shows up briefly at the most inopportune times. Such an encounter occurred during 1992 when we had few contacts with this pod. I finally found them during gale force winds and driving rain while aboard the 42' *Lucky Star*. My crew was asleep, having been up most of the previous night, so with the boat on autopilot I attempted to follow and photograph the whales. I managed to document many but not all of the individuals before putting away the rain soaked camera. They were not seen again that year.

AJ pod consisted of twenty-five whales in 1984; but as of 1992, it had lost two whales and added eight calves. Currently, it has thirty-one members. Initially shy, members of this group have recently begun to approach and follow the research boats. AJ4 has become very friendly and often approaches the boat. It is suspected that this whale may be a maturing female, because females seem to become friendly in the years before producing their first calf. The adult male AJ11, first photographed in 1977, and recently matured male AJ21 are whales that distinguish AJ pod. This pod, most often seen in the late summer and fall, sometimes participates in fall social aggregations with other pods.

Fig-31. AK1, a mature male, has a very distinctive, tall, slender dorsal fin. Photo by Kathy Heise.

Fig-32. AK2, a female, has a distinctive open saddle patch. Compare AK2's dorsal fin with AE10's. Photo by Lance Barrett-Lennard.

AK POD

When photographed in 1983 and 1984, AK pod seemed unusual because of its small size (seven whales) and lack of adult males. However, since then, two males have matured and grown large dorsal fins. The pod has produced five calves, suffered one mortality and now (1993) numbers eleven whales. It is composed of two maternal groups that sometimes travel separately. AK pod often travels alone, although it joins social aggregations in the late summer. The saddle patches of the whales are very scratched, apparently because of frequent rubbing on beaches. They have been photographed rubbing on several beaches including the beach at Point Nowell and the beaches on the west side of Perry Island. When this group is near a beach composed of small rounded gravel, I always hope I will be treated to the rare sight of the whales rubbing. On several occasions I have been rewarded as they rushed toward the shore, turned on their sides and bounced along in the shallows. The AK whales are another pod which includes the Sound in its regular summer range and is normally encountered spring through fall. The tall, thin dorsal fin of AK1 and open saddle patch of the female AK2 identify this pod. They were first photographed in 1983.

Fig-33. The mature male, AN3, has a very distinctive flat topped dorsal fin. Photo by Kathy Heise.

Fig-34. The female, AN10, has distinctive notches at the base of her dorsal fin. Photo by Kathy Heise.

AN10 and AN20 PODS

These two pods were considered a single pod of thirty-five whales in 1984. When we first heard the distinctive calls of AN pod, we nicknamed it "Graeme pod." Their whining calls reminded us of Graeme Ellis complaining about the poor quality of some of the photographs we provide him to make identifications. Often, these whales seem to take on the timbre of a bunch of yowling alley cats.

Since 1988, AN10 and AN20 pods (originally considered subpods) have traveled together less than fifty percent of the time and are by Dr. Bigg's definition two separate pods. This splintering of one very large pod into smaller pods may demonstrate a mechanism for new pod formation. The two splinter pods are named after focal matriarchs in each pod.

There were seventeen members of the smaller AN10 pod in 1993. The larger AN20 pod had twenty-nine members when last photographed in 1990. Since 1988, only the smaller AN10 pod has been regularly sighted in the Sound frequently in the company of other pods — especially the AB pod. AN10 pod is distinguished by the large adult male AN3 and the female AN10 which has

Fig-35. The female AN17 (AN20 pod), has an open saddle patch and small nick in her dorsal fin. Photo by Craig Matkin.

Fig-36. AN25 (AN20 pod), has a blunt-topped dorsal fin with two distinctive dents. Photos by C. Matkin.

distinctive notches at the base of her dorsal fin. One male in this group (AN1) has a collapsed dorsal fin.

It appears that the AN20 pod now centers its range outside the Sound. It is identified by the notched fin adult male AN25 and female AN17 which has an open saddle patch. Members of both AN10 and AN20 pods were first photographed in the Sound in 1977.

AT1 GROUP

In 1984, the year of our first systematic attempt to photograph all the killer whale pods of Prince William Sound, our very first encounter was with this group. Kirsten Englund and I struggled with unfamiliar recording equipment and a new camera setup, unaware that most of the AT1 group was present. This was the largest aggregation of transient whales we have ever photographed together at one time, and these often silent whales were actively vocalizing. Our pictures and recordings were not the best but provided a starting point for future study. At the time, we had no idea of the uniqueness of this encounter.

Fig-37. AT1, a mature male, has a prominent saddle patch extends forward to near the fin's leading edge. Photo by Kathy Heise.

Fig-38. AT10 has a chubby dorsal fin. The saddle patch is much larger than those of residents. Photo by Kathy Heise.

Although members of this group, such as the distinctive AT10 and AT1 are often sighted, none of the twenty-one whales in this group have ever been noted associating with resident pods or with other transients. Members of this group are observed in various sized aggregations which usually number between one and seven individuals, although larger aggregations are sometimes seen. The twenty-one AT1 whales are encountered much more frequently than the transients of British Columbia and Washington State. The AT1s tend to travel in small groups with fluid memberships but only with other AT1 whales. Furthermore, their common calls, which have been studied in detail by Eva Saulitis in her Master's thesis, are distinct from the calls of all other whales roaming the Sound. The uniqueness of this group of whales remains an enigma to whale researchers. Their social structure remains unclear and is currently under study. Future genetic studies may shed some light on their uniqueness and their relationship to other resident and transient whales of the Sound. These are whales have been repeatedly observed feeding on harbor seals, Dall's and harbor porpoise.

Chapter 5: Vocalizations and Echolocation

It was the end of a successful field season and a long day photographing a "superpod" of about seventy killer whales. My wife, Olga, stopped the boat in the midst of the milling whales and dropped the hydrophone over the side. I slipped on the headphones and relaxed on deck in the glow of the sunset. The cacophony of sounds that came from below contrasted dramatically with the calm surface of the sea. A repeated clicking of echolocation sounds rapidly grew louder. Knowing a whale must be getting close, we peered over the side. Through clear water we saw the whale racing toward the boat. The clicking grew in intensity until BANG!!! I threw the headphones off. The whale had rammed the hydrophone! In years of research this had never happened. Surprisingly, the hydrophone was not destroyed. We hoped the whale's curiosity was satisfied.

From the beginning of our research, killer whale calls have repeatedly excited our curiosity and imaginations. The range and variety of resident whale call patterns and the eerie wail of the lone transient whale never cease to captivate us, no matter how many times we hear them. In trying to better understand these exciting vocalizations, we must consider their possible functions. The development of these complex acoustic systems seems to be directly related to the physical properties of the killer whales' environment.

Because water absorbs light more readily than the atmosphere, visibility under water is limited. Plankton and other suspended material serve to further increase the ocean's opacity. However, sound travels about five times faster in water than in air, and its intensity is far less diminished over distance. Consequently, vocalization and listening have become highly specialized in the killer whale, while the importance of vision has diminished, except at close range and near or above the surface. The lobes of

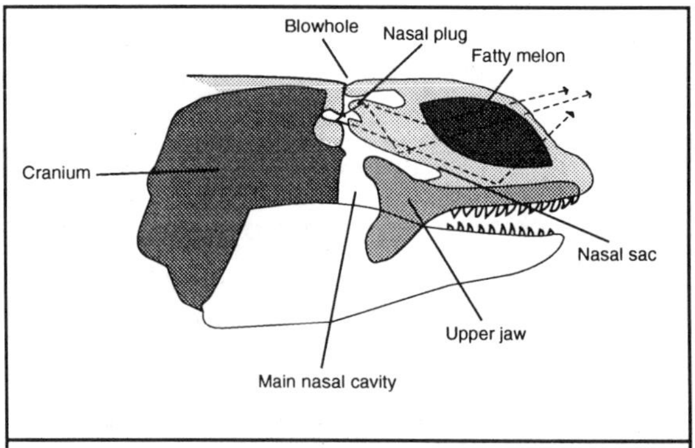

Fig-39. Sound projection in the killer whale. Echolocation. Killer whales transmit clicks through the fatty tissue in the melon. After Hoyt, courtesy of K. Nagahama, illustrator.

the killer whale's brain which are responsible for listening are enlarged reflecting the whale's ability to interpret a wide variety of sounds.

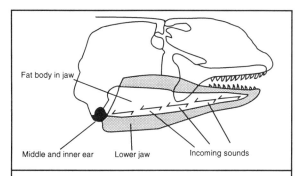

Fat body in jaw

Middle and inner ear   Lower jaw   Incoming sounds

Fig-40. Hearing in the killer whale. Clicks, reflected back by objects in the water, are received through the lower jaw. After Hoyt, courtesy of K. Nagahama illustrator.

Like other toothed whales, killer whales produce two types of vocalizations — one used for echolocation and the other for communication. When echolocating, the whale produces a series of high energy clicks of variable duration that may be repeated up to several hundred times per second.

Echolocation in mammals was first demonstrated in bats which use it to find flying insects at dusk and at night. The blind use echolocation when they walk along tapping a cane listening for changes in sound that occur when they approach solid objects like a wall. However, it was not until the early 1950s that studies of captive bottlenose dolphins demonstrated that they too had a very refined echolocation system. All porpoises, dolphins and other toothed whales apparently use echolocation.

To explore their world with sound, killer whales first produce a rapid series of clicks in the sacs and cavities of their nasal passages. Like all killer whale vocalizations, these clicks are produced without releasing precious air. The high intensity clicks are focused through the fatty tissue (melon) in the forehead of the whale which acts as a sound lens. This beam of sound is directed when the whale rotates its head. The clicks are reflected back by any objects in the water and received through the lower jaw. This lower jaw is filled with an oily substance that conducts the returning sound directly to the inner ear. External ears in killer whales are non-functional pinholes.

One of our crew, Lance Barrett-Lennard, suspects that passive listening, in addition to echolocation, plays a major role in the killer whale's ability to locate and capture prey. It may be that their hearing is so acute that they can detect the movements of prey from a great distance before approaching silently to attack. This seems especially true for the transient whales when they search for seals and porpoises without using echolocation. Transients sometimes use "cryptic clicks" when moving along shorelines. These irregular echolocation clicks may be used for navigation and are often hidden in background noise. Lance has become increasingly concerned that rising levels of noise from boat traffic may interfere with the ability of the whales to listen and find their prey. He feels his own boat may have interrupted hunts for Dall's porpoise on a couple occasions.

Lance finds that resident whales are quite capable of hunting fish without echolocation, yet they have apparently developed a much more complex echolocation system than transients. Evidence suggests that resident whales are very selective when feeding. It appears that a whale may pick out a single king salmon or silver salmon from a mixed school of fish. Sophisticated echolocation would permit the whale to select and follow specific prey long before it could be spotted visually.

To investigate further the use of passive listening and echolocation, Lance has used miles of tape and sophisticated recorders to transcribe acoustic events. This takes hours with the "pickle" down (pickle is whale research jargon for an underwater microphone), drifting, listening and recording while the whales pursue their activities. Sorting out the whales' "acoustic behavior" and relating it to their activities requires patience, a finely tuned ear, and lots of fancy equipment. Fortunately, Lance and Kathy Heise are quite capable of maintaining this delicate equipment and taking the extremely detailed field notes that must accompany their recordings. These two operate as a finely tuned unit keeping

Fig-41. The large bulbous forehead (melon) of the killer whale is a sound focusing lens important for echolocation. Note also the blow hole and white eye patch.

boat, notes and logs, film, and the rest of their equipment in highly organized and perfect working order.

When an underwater microphone (hydrophone) is lowered near a group of resident whales pursuing salmon, one can clearly discern the rapid fire clicks of echolocation. The time between clicks varies becoming shorter when the sound is turned onto nearby objects for detailed examination. Repetition rates of 200 or 300 clicks per second are used for targets at a distance of less than ten feet and may sound like a buzzing. Slow series of one or two clicks per second are probably used to examine targets at a range of 300 to 600 feet. From the returning echoes the whales determine the size, shape and location of an object, its direction of travel and whether or not it is a potential food source. The whales may direct this sound beam at anything, except perhaps each other. Dolphin researcher, Ken Norris, found that in spinner porpoise society it is poor manners to echolocate your schoolmates. Not infrequently, echolocation pulses are directed at or near our boat.

In addition to these high energy clicks, resident whales frequently make an assortment of social calls consisting of squeals, whistles, screams and other repetitive calls. When listening to large groups of these whales underwater, the cacophony conjures visions of beasts from the jungles of Africa roaming the wilderness beneath the waves.

Within the vocabulary of social calls are the discrete calls which seem to be used to identify and locate other pod members. Dr. John Ford, studying these often repetitious and stereotyped calls, has demonstrated that each resident pod in British Columbia and Washington has a repertoire of distinct vocalizations. Each pod's "dialect" distinguishes it from all other pods. Ford suspects that the same may be true for resident pods in the Sound. Major emphasis, in our research, therefore, has been devoted to recording the vocalizations of local resident pods.

There has always been a bit of a friendly division in our research group between the photographers and acoustic researchers. Because the boat must be still with the engine off to collect adequate recordings, it is difficult to gather both photoidentification and acoustical data simultaneously. During our early research, Kirsten Englund would record whale calls from the drifting twenty-six foot research boat while I zipped around in a twelve foot inflatable, snapping identification photographs. If adequate distance was not maintained between the two boats, the whine of the little outboard motor severely intruded on her recordings. Often concentrating on photography, I became oblivious to my location. My close approaches to the boat during recording sessions brought an immediate reaction as Kirsten waved a clenched fist and motioned me to move away — far away. Since then, I have gained the reputation of interfering with and ignoring recordings in pursuit of identification photographs. Dr. Ford remarks with mock seriousness — "Get rid of the fancy camera gear and make more recordings! Acoustics will answer our most important questions!" We have come to recognize the partial truth in his admonitions as we regularly recognize the discrete calls of local pods long before we can see them.

John Ford and Eva Saulitis are carefully defining dialects and examining the acoustic relationship of the pods in the Sound much as Ford did for the pods in British Columbia. As expected, the calls that make up these Prince William Sound dialects are quite distinct from those recorded in British Columbia and Puget Sound.

In British Columbia and Washington, there are distinct northern and southern populations of resident whales which seldom if ever mix. A boundary line seems to exist about halfway up the inside of Vancouver Island. Although the pods within each population share many social calls with each other, there is no sharing of calls between the two groups. Neither population shares calls with the resident pods of Prince William Sound. The Prince William Sound pods share some regional calls, but each pod maintains its own distinctive calls.

Dr. Ford believes the relationship of pods within a population can be determined by the degree to which they share discrete calls. Closely related pods, such as AE and AK, share many discrete calls. Likewise, AB pod (26 whales) and AI pod (6 whales) have similar vocal repertoires. Studying the dialects of local pods, we may be witnessing the final stages of the formation of a new pod as one maternal group (AI pod) becomes independent of the mother pod (AB pod). This gradual process, which may take several generations, should result in the increasing divergence of dialects between the two pods. This is another one of those intriguing questions which further research should be able to resolve.

Acoustic analysis may also be the key to accurately determining interpod relationships. Pods often photographed together may not be closely related acoustically (eg. AB and AN pods) and consequently may not necessarily share a common lineage. Additionally, certain British Columbia pods which seldom interact have been found to share many calls and therefore may be closely related. Dr. Ford calls groups of pods which share calls "acoustic clans."

In many ways, the study of resident social calls dovetails nicely with the findings of our photoidentification work. For example, it supports the photographic evidence that no mixing occurs between resident pods of Prince William Sound and those of British Columbia and Washington State. The striking differences between calls indicate that these populations probably separated long ago and subsequently developed their own unique dialects. Similarly, the pods identified by photography in Prince William Sound can also be distinguished from each other by their discrete calls. Each pod identified photographically has a dialect employing unique calls that distinguish it acoustically from all other pods. Thus, photoidentification and acoustics work together to define pods as social units. A pod's acoustics, which embody a long term record, may even be more useful than photography in tracing historical relationships between pods; only photoidentification, however, can show us the relationships of individual whales within a pod.

In addition to the discrete calls, which serve to identify members of each pod, resident killer whales communicate with an assortment of variable calls and whistles. These most commonly occur when individuals are traveling close together, are at play, or are engaging in sexual or other social activity.

When several resident pods merge and spread out across a broad expanse of water, groups of whales may exhibit different behaviors and hence, may be giving different calls. Some may be feeding, while others are traveling or socializing. The combination of discrete calls, variable calls and whistles, and echolocation pulses sometimes gives the impression of a wild party, each whale attempting to raise his voice above the din.

For years, we have puzzled and puzzled over the banging noises we occasionally hear when resident pods are feeding. At first, we thought they were similar to the "bangs" of sperm whales that Ken Norris describes. He suspects that the sperm whale uses these high intensity sounds to stun its prey. However, Kirsten Englund's analysis of the killer whale bangs indicated they were not similar. John Ford suggested they may be cavitation sounds made by the rapid movement of the whale's flukes. Recently, in their spectacular film "Wolves of the Sea," Dave and Liz Parer-Cook recorded and filmed killer whales underwater stunning herring with rapid slashes of their flukes. The sounds made by the whales' flukes were nearly identical to the puzzling "bangs" we have heard in Prince William Sound.

Humans have long been preoccupied with finding evidence for language similar to our own in dolphins and whales. Although no evidence for such sophisticated linguistic systems have been found, killer whale communication may prove to be quite complex. Adaptations to two very different worlds make comparisons very difficult. Because the natural environment of humans and whales are so different, it is unlikely that analogous communication systems have developed. A whale, for example, performs most of its activities while holding its breath in a world where vision is secondary to hearing.

On the other hand, more information is likely to be contained in the discrete and variable calls of whales than simply the identity and locations of the pod and individuals. Recent studies of other mammals such as Vervet monkeys, suggest that subtle variations in calls may have significant meanings. Often, we have watched an entire traveling pod spread out over a mile synchronously turn and travel in the opposite direction. Some sort of signal is surely involved in coordinating this behavior although no specific call has yet been isolated. Although the whales may not possess a language as humans define it, they seem clearly to transmit more information in their calls than we are able to decipher.

Unlike resident whales which we often locate acoustically, the more silent transients must often be located visually. The acoustic picture is just now beginning to emerge for the less studied transient whales, whose relative silence makes recording difficult. Initially, Eva Saulitis thought the AT1 transients were completely silent while hunting; however, later, she discovered that they made "quiet" calls. She first thought these sounds were being made by the hydrophone itself, but eventually traced them to the whales. Perhaps, these weak calls permit some communication between the foraging whales but are not perceptible to their warm-blooded prey.

The transients most frequently seen in Prince William Sound, the AT1 group, seem to share a dialect of ten calls. They share at least one call with the transients of Southeast Alaska, British Columbia and California. Although these groups apparently no longer mix, the common call suggests a recent connection. The other transients that are

Fig-42. Acoustic monitoring is another non-intrusive method of obtaining valuable information about the killer whales. Often whales are heard before they are seen. Eva Saulitis checks her equipment before placing the hydrophone in the water.

infrequently seen in the Sound have not been recorded, and we have no idea of their acoustical relationship with the Sound's more common transients. This is another research project waiting to be done.

Eva is mapping the vocal repertoire of the AT1 group and relating it to the whales' behaviors. Unlike resident vocalizations, transient calls can be related to specific behaviors. She has categorized hunting calls, social calls, and lone whale calls. The loud, mournful, siren-like tones of lone whales are unique. Lone transients may continue these repetitious calls for hours. The most excited and variable vocalizations come from transient whales after a kill. Some vocalizations border on the bizarre; I have heard some that sound like a phonograph needle being dragged across a record.

Without the ability to listen to the whales' vocalizations, we would be unaware of major facets of their lives. Acoustic equipment for listening to killer whales is relatively inexpensive and is available to the amateur whale watcher. John Ford's wife, Bev, constructs hydrophones in her basement shop.* To aid in locating whales, the hydrophone can be attached to a "directional dish." This piece of equipment need not be elaborate. A large cooking wok with sound absorbing neoprene rubber glued to the backside and a centered mounting bracket for the hydrophone works well. This assembly is lowered beneath the water on a long pole and rotated until the direction of the calls is determined. This simple home made device allows us to detect resident pods at distances up to ten miles, whereas the view from a crows nest thirty feet above the deck of a boat is limited to only a few miles.

One of the great advantages of acoustic study is that there is little danger of harassing the whales. No research permit is required. The boat can be run ahead of the whales, giving them a wide berth, the engines can be stopped, and recordings made as the whales pass by. This gives the whales the option of approaching the vessel, rather than forcing the presence of the boat upon them.

* Bev C. Ford
5454 Indian River Drive
North Vancouver, British Columbia
CANADA V7G 1L3

Chapter 6: Killer Whales and other Marine Mammals

The killer whale has a dual, even contradictory reputation. Captive killer whales appear to be gentle, giant dolphins, while the killer whale of folklore and historical accounts has the reputation of being be an efficient, unflinching predator specializing in warm-blooded prey. What is the true nature of the killer whale? The question is complex and the answers depend in part on which type of killer whale one is describing — residents or transients. Our field observations indicate that wild killer whales are both intelligent, playful, gentle creatures and at the same time highly skilled and efficient predators.

During our early observations, it was a surprise, if not somewhat of a disappointment, to see Dall's porpoise casually mingling with killer whale pods. There were no chases nor kills, and the killer whales seemed to show little interest in the porpoises. It was startling to watch the porpoises speed in to join the rapidly traveling whales. The "rooster tail" splashes of the speeding por-

Fig-43. A Dall's porpoise is bounced into the air during a prolonged attack by transient killer whales. Photo by Eva Saulitis.

Fig-44. "Stevie" the Dall's Porpoise swam with AB pod most of the summer of 1984. He behaved much like the killer whales. Photo by Craig Matkin.

poises marked their advance. The porpoises would often begin riding the bow wave generated by the whales, just as they frequently ride the bow waves of boats. Although this seemed a unique and remarkable observation at the time, it has proven to be a common occurrence — but only between Dall's porpoise and the fish-eating, resident pods.

The most unusual Dall's porpoise/killer whale interaction occurred in 1984 between a single, full-grown porpoise (we nicknamed it "Stevie") and AB pod. From late June until late September, when the field season ended, "Stevie" swam with AB pod. The porpoise had unique scratches and markings that made

Fig-45. "Stevie" had distinguishing marks on his/her side that made reidentification possible. Photo by Olga von Ziegezar.

it possible to repeatedly identify it among its whale friends. Not only did it swim with the killer whales, it began to act like a miniature killer whale. Rather than surfacing quickly or arching his tail stock as Dall's porpoises normally do, this wayward porpoise extended its back "killer whale style" lengthening its time at the surface. Stevie also tended to mimic the breathing rate of the whales around him, and when the whales arched and dove deep it imitated their actions. The whales seemed quite accepting of Stevie's presence, and it was often difficult to believe that this porpoise with similar black and white markings was not just a dwarf killer whale. In 1985, searching through AB pod and the other pods, we discovered that "Stevie" the wayward porpoise had disappeared. Perhaps, it returned to its own kind, or maybe it tried to get friendly with some marine mammal eating, transient killer whales and became a winter meal. Why it began swimming with AB pod remains a mystery. However, the last place a group of transient whales would look for a Dall's porpoise probably would be among a group of resident killer whales!

There is no doubt that Dall's porpoises are food for transient killer whales in Prince William Sound. In 1978 during a land-based study, all whales were counted as they passed by our shore camp on Squire Island. Here we found the first evidence of the importance of the Dall's porpoise to the diet of the killer whale. From the high bluff above the camp, we watched a group of five killer whales "playing" with several Dall's porpoise. From our elevated vantage point, we watched the twisting and turning of the porpoises in the clear water as they dove in front of the whales. There was no obvious signs of an attack, so we considered this a brief and benign encounter. However, this observation proved to be in error; for a short time later, evidence to the contrary washed up on the cobble beach below the bluff. The head of a Dall's porpoise calf neatly severed from its body lay among the stones.

Eva Saulitis, Lance Barrett-Lennard, and Kathy Heise have spent many hours following the more elusive transient killer whales and have observed further examples of transient predation. In one encounter, Eva watched a group of four whales pursue a Dall's porpoise. First, they chased it as it zigzagged at the surface and then followed it as it dove below. When the hapless porpoise resurfaced, the whales rammed it repeatedly sending it flying into the air several times before it disappeared. On another occasion, a group of killer whales rapidly charged in on a porpoise. An explosion of bubbles came to the surface followed by a cloud of blood. Another porpoise was chased for five minutes at high speed before it suddenly disappeared.

The harbor porpoise, although less abundant in the Sound in the summer also appears to be a common prey of transient killer whales. One day Lance and Kathy watched two killer whales charge by, then make a long dive that was followed by vigorous splashing when one whale resurfaced. Milling birds and an oily slick marked the spot. As they approached the scene, a pair of harbor porpoise lungs floated to the surface. Kathy deftly retrieved them. She gasped when she realized the head with the skin neatly peeled off was still attached.

The mature Steller sea lion with its aggressive manner and formidable teeth is not a passive prey for transient whales. A 1000 pound sea lion with a skull and jaw much like that of a brown bear is not a creature to be taken lightly. Although they probably occur with some regularity, only a single well-documented attack on a Steller sea lion by killer whales has been observed in the Sound. On this occasion, Karl Becker watched four killer whales circle a dozen, nervous, tightly grouped sea lions. One smaller sea lion became separated from the rest of the group and immediately a large male killer whale knifed between it and the other sea lions. The whale seemed to follow the single sea lion as it quickly dove. The sea lion flippers appeared briefly, with the whale alongside, then sank out of sight. All four whales appeared and moved about 100 meters away where they milled at the surface. An oily sheen appeared, and gulls flew above the whales. Karl idled over and watched the gulls feed on sea lion "crumbs" as he called the bits of fat and small blood clots that remained on the water's surface.

Although there are haulouts inside the Sound where larger sea lions aggregate, there is a lack of rookeries to provide vulnerable youngsters. It is probably pups and young sea lions that are taken most frequently by the whales. Stomachs of killer whales from the Sound have yielded primarily the remains of pups or young sea lions (see Behavior-feeding). In British Columbia one method used by transient whales when attacking sea lions is to swim rapidly past and strike at the sea lion with a slash of their powerful flukes. It may take many passes to immobilize a sea lion. Until the sea lion is immobilized, the whales are careful to keep lips and eyes away from the sea lion's powerful jaws. It is possible that some of the gashes, nicks and scratches on the fins of transients come from encounters with sea lions.

British Columbia researchers have also observed transient whales using this fluke slashing technique in attacking harbor seals. More typically, a harbor seal is dispatched quickly underwater followed by rapid milling of the whales at the surface. The only evidence of the kill may be an oil slick and bits of hair or flesh that rise to the surface to be grabbed by hovering gulls. On a recent trip to British Columbia, Graeme and I spent part of a day following three transient killer whales which consumed at least three harbor seals over the course of a single afternoon.

Resident killer whales occasionally exhibit a different relationship to Steller sea lions than do transients. Typically, they show little interest in one another, except when both whales and sea lions are feeding in the same location and possibly on the same prey. Perhaps because of competition for food, sea lions have been observed chasing resident killer whales nipping at their flukes to the obvious irritation of the whales. On one occasion, Graeme and I watched a large male killer whale (AB3) resting on his side after some long feeding dives. Two sea lions feeding in the same area moved in and one nipped the whale on the belly. The whale nearly hopped out of the water and then shot rapidly away. The sea lion resurfaced belching and growling.

There have been reports of attacks on larger baleen whales; however, none of our group has observed such behavior. Apparently attacks on large whales in the Sound are rare occurrences. However, the distinctive killer whale tooth marks can be seen on some humpback whales. These encounters may have occurred elsewhere. It has been hypothesized that specific groups of transient killer whales may specialize in feeding on particular marine mammals.

Fig-46. Killer whales have inflicted considerable damage on this humpback whale's tail flukes. Note the parallel teeth marks that are typically left by killer whales. Photo by Craig Matkin.

Chapter 7: Killer Whale Behaviors

Because whales spend most of their lifetime beneath the waves where they are not easily observed, their behavior is difficult to study. Furthermore, the snippets of behavior that occur at the ocean's surface may not be representative of the animals' behavior below and are not always easy to interpret. To further complicate the picture, various subgroups of a large group of resident whales spread out across a passage may be involved in different behaviors at the same moment. For example, a group of juveniles may be playing while another trio of adults is resting half a mile away. At present, the critical examination of whale behavior is still in its infancy.

Based on observation, broad categories of behavior have been identified. Major behavioral categories include traveling, foraging and feeding, resting (group resting and individual resting), and social interaction/play. These are general categories used for many animal behavior studies. Although resident and transient whales share many of these behaviors, there are significant differences between the two types. Eva Saulitis is presently taking a closer look at some of the behaviors peculiar to transient whales.

Traveling

Both resident and transient killer whales are constantly on the move. The fabric of their lives is woven with the thread of constant motion. Even during resting, there is often some degree of steady movement. With an average speed of about three knots, they may

Fig-47. A roving group of transient killer whales charges up alongside the NGOS skiff. Notice the large nick in the dorsal fin of the whale on the far left. Photo by C. Matkin.

cover considerable distances during a twenty-four hour period. At times, whales move back and forth through the same areas for several days. Thus, whale researchers must distinguish this behavior from true "traveling behavior" where the basic activity is moving from point A to point B. In true traveling, no feeding, social activity or resting are observed. During slow travel the whales swim only two to three knots. However, during spurts of rapid travel, they have been clocked at eight to ten knots. Typically, a traveling resident whale will breathe three or four times while moving along at the surface and then make a three to five minute dive. After the last breath, the whale makes a slight arch of the back and tail stock as it begins to sound. The whale moves faster while submerged and will resurface to repeat the same breathing and diving pattern. Transients make dives as long as ten minutes while traveling. Traveling occupies over thirty percent of their time while this figure seems to be much less for resident whales. In the Sound transients may have to travel great distances to find prey (porpoise and seals) scattered over a wide area.

Killer whales traveling in small groups afford the best opportunity for obtaining identification photographs. On one occasion we followed AB pod as it steadily crossed the Sound, traveling over forty-five nautical miles in ten hours. On another occasion, AK pod was photographed near Fairmont Island then photographed again twenty-three hours later near Chenega Point — 42 miles to the southwest.

Occasionally, transient whales have been observed swimming at great speed. Often this occurs when whales are about to join another group. We have clocked them porpoising along at the surface at 16 knots for short periods. Shooting alongside a formation of speed swimming killer whales in a

Fig-48. Part of the largest group of resting assemblage we have seen. About 80 whales from three pods were abreast in group resting formation. Photo by Craig Matkin.

small skiff, one is mesmerized by the full extent of their strength and power. Their blows explode as they break the surface, and the spray flies as their bulk hurtles forward, half their body breaking free of the water.

Often young whales will swing into ride on our stern wake, speed swimming in toward the skiff or boat and then surfing along in the rapidly foaming wake. Once a nearly thirty foot long adult male actually swung alongside the thirty-six foot research vessel and swam along in the bow wake for a short period. These behaviors serve as reminders that the killer whale is really a very large dolphin.

Resting

Killer whales cannot settle down for a good night's sleep as we do. Their breathing, unlike ours, is voluntary which means they must consciously rise to the surface to breathe. Resting seems to be a ritualized pod activity. Often whales in a pod will synchronize movements and breathing patterns when they slow their activities to a rest. When "group resting," all or part of a pod assemble into a tight unit. Movements are slow with a series of up to ten breaths taken before the animals arch and submerge for four to ten minutes. The whales keep moving slowly, sometimes back and forth in the same area. As resting deepens, the movements of the whales become slower, and the time they spend submerged increases. There is little vocalization other than distinct and infrequent resting calls. During group resting, the whales may shun interaction with vessels. If approached, they tend to circle away from the boat.

During group resting, whales frequently line up in their maternal groups. The relationships between the individuals are clearly defined. A mother and her offspring often rest shoulder to shoulder with the youngest offspring closest to the mother. Even the order in which the whales surface appears to be highly ritualized.

Occasionally, more than one pod rests together. Once, we observed more than seventy whales (AN and AJ pods) stretching in a line, shoulder to shoulder, resting in a single group. Their dorsal fins were lined up like pickets in a fence as the whales surfaced together. Group resting may continue for three or four hours, although usually it occurs for shorter periods.

Often the calves do not seem as interested in resting as the adults and will continue to play as the others begin to rest. On one occasion, a frolicking calf rolled repeatedly over its mother's back while the pod moved slowly. The vocalizations of the calf continued as the other whales fell silent. Suddenly, there was sharp call and a slap of the mother's flukes. The calf made a noise like a squealing pig and darted off. Then, quietly it returned and lined up alongside its mother.

Group resting occupies a significant percentage of the whales' time (probably over ten percent). This indicates the importance of this activity. It may be a time when social bonds are strengthened as indicated by the ritualized nature of the activity.

"Individual resting" more closely resembles sleep in humans, although it hardly seems more than a catnap by our standards. When resting individually, a whale hangs motionless in the water with blowhole and dorsal fin exposed. It may remain motionless for one to three minutes before rising slightly and breathing. Finally, as it begins to sink below the surface, the whale wakes and either resumes its resting position or begins to move along in the water again. Individual resting may involve a single whale or a small group of whales. It is the only time that these whales seem to stop moving.

Whales in the AT1 transient group mostly rest individually and have only been seen group resting on rare occasions. However, Eva once watched transients group resting for over seven hours in Dangerous Passage, behind Chenega Island.

Foraging and Feeding

During spring and summer when millions of herring and salmon return to the Sound, both residents and transients spend much of their time foraging and feeding. However, their feeding techniques and targeted prey are quite different.

The first schooling fish to arrive in the Sound are the herring. In late March and April, they rise from deep water areas and prepare for their spring spawning preferring particular intertidal areas in the northern and eastern Sound and along Montague Island. Unlike salmon that die after spawning once, herring return to spawn annually from an age of three or four years until they die. Some herring survive to an age of ten years or more. Up to 100,000 tons or about 600 million of these small silvery fish may rise from the depths where they overwinter and enter the Sound's shallower waters. Although snow may still be piled along the tideline and the brisk winter winds may still blow, the return of the herring marks the end of the long, lean, winter; and every predator from bald eagles, to shorebirds, diving ducks, sea lions, whales and humans congregate to take advantage of the sudden abundance.

At this time of year, the resident whales often cruise the areas south of Naked Island in the central Sound, where huge schools of herring stage before dispersing to spawn. The herring are still deep in the water column at 300 feet or more so we cannot observe the whales preying on them. However, the whales' breath smells distinctly of herring and their four to five minute long dives strongly suggest diving to these depths. Also, echolocation clicks and discrete calls suggest feeding.

While the resident pods follow the herring in the central Sound, the transients are seen inshore along the spawning beaches. It is not herring that interests them, but the harbor seals and Steller sea lions that follow the ripe, egg-filled fish.

In the Sound, killer whales begin feeding on salmon as early as mid-May. The whales seem particularly excited by the arrival of these early salmon. Leaping and splashing whales and salmon hurtling through the air may be part of these early feeding bouts. Once an excited young whale rocketed in next to the boat, breached with a salmon crosswise in its jaws, then briefly placed the fish beside the boat before grabbing it again and blasting off through the waves. The whale's intent seemed to be to show off its prize.

Various stocks of salmon enter the Sound regularly throughout the summer. Some pods may begin feeding on salmon in May by intercepting the red and king salmon runs on the adjacent Copper River Delta. The largest regular returns are the millions of pink salmon that enter via the southwestern entrances in July and August. In early September killer whale predation on salmon generally ends, because the numbers of returning fish dwindle.

As the fish enter the passages leading into the Sound, the whales spread out moving down the passages to intercept them. Although there have been accounts of entire pods cooperating in hunting salmon, we have not observed this behavior. Most frequently, single whales are seen chasing and eating the fish. However, groups of two or three whales sometimes work together. While fishing, the whales may be spread out for a mile or more across a channel. When a whale locates a group of fish, a twisting, circling pursuit generally ensues. The chase starts below the surface: the whale circles the fish and drives them toward the surface. It ends as the whale shoots through the school grabbing a fish. Often the arched back of a lunging, twisting whale breaks the surface. Occasionally, a whale breaks the water with a salmon clasped in its jaws. At other times, scales from the salmon floating near the surface are all that mark the site of a successful hunting foray.

When possible, we hurry to the site of a kill and sieve the water with a fine mesh net to capture drifting fish scales. The scales provide concrete evidence of salmon predation and allow us to determine the specific species preyed upon.

During September and October, large groups of socializing resident killer whale pods sometimes congregate in the western Sound to feed on herring. The herring appear in small schools near the surface and can be seen flipping and finning on calm days. Occasionally, a whale will surface with herring spurting from its mouth. When herring are abundant, Steller sea lions may feed side by side with the whales.

There is little doubt that killer whales eat a wide variety of foods but little is known of their feeding habits in Prince William Sound — especially their winter diet. On one occasion, we observed sandlance or needlefish, a three to four inch fish no wider than a pencil, streaming from the mouths of a pair of resident killer whales. These fish are so small and thin that one would think they would slip out between the whale's teeth! It is likely the whales also feed on gray cod, halibut and possibly squid. Except for halibut taken from the longlines of fishermen, we have not observed whales feeding on these species. However, these species have been found in killer whale stomachs from other areas. We have seen killer whales deep diving in areas where halibut and other bottomfish are known to be abundant.

Transient killer whales usually prey on larger, warm-blooded animals. However, on rare occasions, they have been seen pursuing salmon. It is not known whether there is a seasonality to their feeding habits. During the summer and fall, they prey on harbor porpoise, Dall's porpoise and harbor seals. The more robust Steller sea lion is another likely prey, although we have not observed killer whales attacking sea lions in the Sound. In 1992, Eva Saulitis found tags from thirteen Steller sea lion pups in an adult male killer whale carcass on Montague Island. The pups had been tagged on Marmot Island in 1987 and 1988 over two hundred miles to the southwest. Although we have never seen it ourselves, we have two reports by reliable observers of killer whales attacking minke whales in Prince William Sound. Such attacks have been reported from other areas in Alaska.

There also are rare reports of killer whales attacking sea otters, although we have never seen it, despite the frequent proximity of sea otters and transient whales. Since sea otters use fur as a primary insulator, rather than fat like most marine mammals, their food-value for whales may be low. Fat has the highest energy content of foods, which may explain the why killer whales rip the oil rich tongue from the baleen whale before the carcass sinks and why AB pod is so intent on removing the oil rich blackcod from fishermen's lines.

For years, there were few observations of marine mammal kills by transient whales. It took years to develop the experienced eye needed to observe these kills. Most attacks occur beneath the surface so confirming a kill requires tuning in on the proper clues such as a bit of floating seal fur, a telltale oil slick, or birds grabbing a small chunk of porpoise blubber. The rapid milling at the surface and loud vocalizations that often follow a kill provide further clues. Sometimes, we have observed several attacks on marine mammals in rapid succession. More often, we spend long hours watching transient whales forage into small bays and passages with only the rare sign of a successful kill.

Surface Behavior

Killer whales express themselves in a wide variety of surface behaviors. The most dramatic is the full breach, when the whale rockets free of the water to land on its side with a great splash. The whales practice every form of breaching imaginable, from grand belly or back flops to weak lunges with only the forward part of the body leaving the water. Most of this type of activity occurs during play and social sessions; although, it may occur during feeding bouts as well. Breaching may be used by transients to stun their marine mammal prey.

Lobtailing and flipper slapping are also common surface behaviors. When lobtailing the whale repeatedly slaps the tail flukes on the surface of the water. The whale may be in either a belly down or belly up position. When flipper slapping, the whale

Fig- 49. Two male killer whales frolic. The whale on the left is spyhopping, while the one on the right is lobtailing. Note the large flippers and downcurved tail flukes. Photo by Eva Saulitis.

rolls on its side and repeatedly slaps one foreflipper on the surface. The whale may exhibit these behaviors while stationary or moving along at the surface.

These types of surface activity generally reflect a high level of excitement. It may be that the sound of the surface splashes is used to communicate with other nearby whales. Dr. Kenneth Norris believes that aerial behavior and splashes of spinner dolphins define the boundaries of the school. However, this may not be true for the often widespread groups of resident killer whales because the sound of a breaching or tail slapping often travels only a short distance underwater. Furthermore, resident killer whales possess well-developed vocabularies of discrete calls that may be more effective in communicating their location.

Since calves and juveniles indulge in these activities more than adults, we suspect that often they may be a form of play. Young whales seem to get great pleasure out of creating new styles of breaching or slapping. This play may be an effective means of enhancing young whales' agility and muscle tone, thereby improving their hunting abilities. Also, it may cement the social bonds that are essential for the pod's operation.

Both resident and transient whales may exhibit any of these surface behaviors, although they are seen with greater regularity in resident pods. The stealthy hunting behavior of transients in pursuit of marine mammals may preclude behaviors that alert others to their presence. Transients occasionally exhibit surface behaviors during or following kills or during intense social activity.

Spyhopping represents a final type of surface behavior exhibited by Prince William Sound killer whales. I am always surprised when a killer whale abruptly shoves its head and upper body vertically out of the water, eyes clearly exposed, and then slowly and gently slides back into the depths. When this occurs nearby, the unexpected eye contact with the whale can be quite startling. This spyhopping behavior appears to be the whale's method of determining its position relative to boats and other surface phenomena. The killer whale seems to have reasonably good vision when out of the water. No doubt, the whale's natural curiosity also helps to account for this spyhopping behavior. We have often witnessed whales spyhopping when approached by boats, especially at times when whales are socializing or moving erratically at the surface. Once a young whale spyhopped three times consecutively about fifty feet from the boat. Apparently, one look at us and our equipment was not sufficient to satisfy his curiosity.

The most exciting times to observe resident whales is during periods of spirited play and social activity. Frequently, these sessions occur after feeding. At such times, we observe the most breaching (leaping from the water), lobtailing (slapping of the tail on the water) and flipper slapping (rolling on the side and slapping the foreflipper repeatedly on the water). Most of the activity occurs beneath the surface so we can only guess at what is happening and its significance.

There seems to be a general increase in the amount of socializing at the end of the summer season and in the fall when the whales appear to be well fed. During late August and September, up to six pods and over one hundred and twenty whales may mix and socialize in Montague Strait or Lower Knight Island Passage. Sexual activity often occurs.

The most frequently observed sexual activity involves two or more males. Very seldom are young or mature females involved. It is always surprising to watch large adult males with penis extended mounting (from beneath) and cavorting with immature males. Perhaps, as suggested by Dr. Norris for the spinner porpoise, much of the perceived sexual activity helps reaffirm the social network within the pod. It also may establish social hierarchies among males. Perhaps, lack of participation by mature females is due to their more serious leadership role. Do the seemingly serious females lead the pod while the young and mature males lag behind rolling and slapping flippers with large pink penises exposed? Perhaps male-female sexual activity is simply very sedate in comparison with the male displays and draws little attention. Sexual activity in vertebrates (i.e. many birds, elephant seals, sea lions) often involves highly ritualized and flamboyant displays and aggressive interactions that culminate in relatively mundane matings. With killer whales the role of many social behaviors are simply not understood.

Although sexual activity may occur at any time of year, actual matings between adult whales are very rarely observed. We suspect that most successful breedings occur in the fall. This timing, coupled with the known seventeen month gestation period established by monitoring captive whales, would produce the observed winter and spring births.

Researchers have often questioned the role of the adult male's large dorsal fin, huge rounded front flippers and downcurved fluke tips. Graeme Ellis suggests this well-developed sexual dimorphism in males is related to their mating behavior. During mating, the male swims beneath the female and turns upside down. He slowly rises beneath her and cradles her between his very large foreflippers. When upside down, the dorsal fin seems to work like the keel of a sailboat to keep him from rolling from side to side. The stabilizing effect of the dorsal fin may be especially important for this species which seems to do everything while on the move. The downcurved flukes fit over the females flukes to help hold her steady. The few instances where we believe actual mating has been observed seem to support this theory. Male killer whales mount other males in a similar fashion. If this theory is true it raises the question of the effect of the collapsed dorsal fins of AB2, AB3, and AN1 on their ability to successfully mate.

During rough play sessions, there is often much mouthing particularly among young males and calves. Most of the scratches and marks used to identify individual whales are tooth marks made by other killer whales. Young males seem to have far more of these marks than adult and female whales. However, some newborn calves are also heavily marked and scarred, possibly indicating a difficult birth.

The time spent in social activity is much less for transient whales than for residents. This may reflect the need of transients to conserve energy for the greater amount of traveling and foraging required to find food.

Beach Rubbing

My wife Olga and I had been following AB pod for most of the afternoon. The whales are approaching Point Grace at the north end of Latouche Island when five whales suddenly veer into Sleepy Bay. Slicing along at high speed, it appears they are about to beach themselves. They roll on their sides blow out a stream of bubbles and flop along parallel to the beach in only a few feet of water. Finally it dawns on us that these whales are beach-rubbing. This behavior is common in Johnstone Strait in Canada; but until that day, we had not observed it in Prince William Sound.

Killer whales are often observed beach-rubbing in British Columbia. One particular beach in Robson Bight on Vancouver Island has become renowned for the repeated, often daily rubbing of killer whales on its cobbles. This behavior seems to be an integral part of the everyday activities of these whales and only specific beaches are used.

In contrast, Prince William Sound killer whales seem to prefer any one of a number of beaches; and for most pods, bouts of rubbing occur infrequently. Known rubbing beaches are scattered throughout the Sound and include: two areas on the west side of Perry Island, the beach at Point Nowell, a beach in

Sleepy Bay on Latouche Island, a beach in Mummy Cove (Knight Island), one in Port Valdez, and beaches in Port Fidalgo and Eaglek. Rubbing beaches, composed of round pebbles a couple inches or less in diameter, are generally of moderate slope.

Not all pods photographed in the Sound have been observed rubbing, and some whales seem more fond of it than others. The whales of AK pod (a group of 11 whales) are most frequently seen rubbing. Some of their white saddle patches are noticeably scratched by the pebbles, facilitating their identification. Some members of AB pod also seem particularly fond of rubbing.

Often the whales dart onto a rubbing beach on their way through an area, spend a few minutes rubbing, then move on their way again. As they approach the shallow beach underwater, fountains of bubbles rise to the surface. Each whale exhales to lose buoyancy before turning on its side and moving into the shallows. Sometimes foreflippers are seen waving in the air as the whales bump along the bottom.

Rubbing may help to remove parasites. Although killer whales are generally free of obvious external parasites, small parasites, flush with the skin have been found on the flanks of some beached whales. Alternatively, rubbing may also be a way of sloughing old skin. Or, it may have some social function, particularly in British Columbia where it seems a ritualized cultural activity for some pods. Another motivation may be that it just plain feels good. Whales are particularly sensitive to disturbance on rubbing beaches and may leave the area if boats approach.

Close encounters with the whales

Initially, we were extremely concerned that our close approach to the whales for photography would disturb them. However, our consistent, careful technique has resulted in their habituation to our research vessels. As the major resident pods have been followed, photographed, and observed, they have gradually became easier to work with. At times, they even seem to enjoy our company. Although some pods, notably AB and AI pods, have been tolerant and curious from the beginning, others, such as AE pod, were initially very difficult to approach. If not feeding or otherwise preoccupied, the major resident pods, AB, AI, AN, AJ, AK, and AE will now allow very close approach for photographs. In fact, they often swim too near for proper identification photographs. Of course, any close approach of whales for photographs requires a research permit. Even though permitted, we are careful not to harass the whales. Sometimes we joke that it is the whales who "harass" us by playing with the skiff and not permitting us to position the skiff for proper photographic angles!

Transient whales are often more difficult to approach, perhaps because they need to be secretive when hunting marine mammals. The sound of a boat nearby may not be appreciated by the whales. However, even the stealthy transients at times can be surprisingly tolerant. Occasionally, they are easy to approach and on rare occasions will approach or swim under the boat.

The residents are generally more friendly than the transients. In 1984 three AB pod whales — AB16, AB19, and AB23 — were the first whales to initiate a friendship with us. These young whales seemed fascinated by the orange inflatable that was towed behind our boat and would follow it for long periods of time. If we put a person in it, all the better. They would roll up and look at us before surfacing just out of arm's reach.

The most striking example of a friendly killer whale was AB8, a young female. Often, she could be seen charging across toward the boat, leaving her pod-mates, and staying with us for hours on end as we paralleled the course of the rest of the pod. She loved to porpoise along in our stern wake when we ran at higher speeds. She would sometimes get right up in the propeller wash for a "whale jacuzzi;" so we nicknamed this whale "Bubbles." Her prop watching habit has since been picked up by many other whales. It seems they either enjoy the bubbling effect or are entranced by the pattern of the turning prop.

When we stopped, Bubbles would often swim circles around the boat; pausing, she seemed to wonder why we were sitting around. Sometimes I would stop and put on a face mask. When I leaned over the side, she would rise up beneath to look at me nose to nose, turning her head to size me up with first one eye then the other. She would always back slightly out of range if I reached out to touch her.

At times, she followed the boat until we completed our research apparently unconcerned about the other whales. On one of these occasions, I slipped into the water with her. A human flopping ungracefully in the water is apparently boring or displeasing to a killer whale. She soon became disinterested. I grabbed on to the stern of the inflatable and was towed slowly along behind the boat. With this she became fascinated and excitedly swam along beside and beneath me. Bubbles used only a gentle motion of her flukes to glide along at three knots (cruising speed for a killer whale); the seeming effortlessness of her movements was remarkable. She would always rise to breathe in the same position in relation to the inflatable, much as she would rise in the same position in relation to the other whales in her maternal group. On several occasions she swam beneath me upside down giving the impression she was about to lift me out of the water on her belly. This was a rare situation and occurred only because of a unique, long-term relationship that had been established with this whale. And, it was a relationship that had been initiated by the whale.

On one occasion, Bubbles refused to leave the boat and actually followed us into our anchorage. Because the pod by this time was miles away, we felt obliged to head back out and return her to her pod (although I am sure she was quite capable of finding her own way back!). Eventually, Bubbles began showing up with a juvenile, AB12, and together they would race circles around the boat, leap at our bow and spend considerable time, snout just inches behind the prop, "prop watching." This behavior makes us nervous, but the whales seem in complete control and have yet to make a mistake.

As Graeme Ellis predicted, AB8 soon had a calf and became less interested in our company. For unknown reasons, it seems that young females, on the verge of becoming mothers, are most likely to become friendly. Currently, AJ4 and AN12 have picked up friendly habits; and although their sex is yet undetermined, their friendliness suggests that they are young females.

Unfortunately, both AB8 and AB12 are now dead. These highly atypical deaths of a juvenile and a young mother are very disturbing. AB12 died in 1986 after exhibiting bullet wounds apparently suffered during interactions with the blackcod fishery. AB8 died at the time of the *Exxon Valdez* Oil Spill leaving an orphan calf, AB41 who was still alive in 1993.

Even the more aloof, hard to approach transient killer whales can sometimes turn unexpectedly friendly. A

Fig-50. Bubbles swims in the research vessel's propwash.

most striking example occurred in Montague Strait where Eva Saulitis and I made the first encounter with the transient AT60 group. It was Eva's first trip out and her first encounter with whales from our 20 foot open, photoidentification skiff. From their swimming behavior and the shapes of the dorsal fins, I knew these were transient whales. Confidently, I told Eva that these whales would be difficult to approach — especially since we had never encountered this group before. Quite to the contrary, two of the females (or subadult males) swung rapidly over in our direction and under our skiff. One then drew up abreast and began breaching alongside. We slowed the skiff and tried to maneuver away from the whales to get identification pictures. They moved with us, so we slowed to a stop. One whale stopped abruptly alongside. When Eva moved to that side of the skiff, the whale breached and sent a shower of water toward her. She moved quickly out of the way and to the other side of the skiff. The whale followed her, repeated the breach, and again sprayed her — this time almost soaking her. The whale's behavior was clearly no accident. It was now swimming tight circles around the skiff breaching again and again in an attempt to soak Eva with a well-directed shower. At this point, Eva did not seem impressed by my ability to predict transient whale behavior. We motored forward. The whale followed. As we sped up, the whale began to swim in our stern wake and repeatedly breached toward the stern of the skiff, landing but a few feet behind us and quite intentionally sending a shower of spray into the boat. This was becoming a bit disconcerting, especially, since we had never seen these whales before. Two of the whales were now in front of our 42' mothership, *F.V. Lucky Star*, with their flukes in the air, waving them in the wind and occasionally slapping the water. Repeatedly, they crisscrossed back and forth under the boat. Finally, as they swam abreast down the Strait, we hesitantly followed to get our photographs.

Despite these types of encounters, even the well-known resident pods do not always tolerate our presence. Generally, determining when we are unwanted is not difficult. Once, while following a mother and young calf, the two whales suddenly turned abruptly and charged toward our 14' inflatable, swam beneath it and lunged in front of us. The mother's flukes just barely grazed the bow of the inflatable. She slapped the water twice with her flukes to make sure we got the hint; then the pair moved rapidly away. The message was clear. She may have been nursing the calf when we approached and was not pleased at being disturbed. Although cows are not generally overprotective of their calves and do not object to an approach, they must be approached cautiously and with consideration. It is not unusual for a calf to spurt away from its mother and swim along with the research boat as mother swims nearby.

Transients are most easily harassed. They often become so elusive that pictures are difficult or impossible to obtain. Sometimes, they have openly demonstrated their displeasure. In one instance, we had been persistently dogging the path of several transients, including a pair of large males. Finally, we got abreast of them and prepared to take photographs. One male, probably 30 feet long and 6 tons in weight swung in near our 26 foot boat and rocketed into the air, his whole body airborne. We winced at the impact of his body on the water and ducked to avoid the spray. To emphasize the point, he launched his body a second time and a bit closer. There was a gasp as his tonnage smacked the surface. Immediately, we backed off, way off! Suddenly the identification pictures did not seem quite so important!

Lance Barrett-Lennard believes transient killer whales rely on passive listening to find their warm-blooded prey. This may make them more sensitive to boat noise and the close approach of vessels. Whale watchers should be aware of these whales and their possible sensitivity to underwater noise. When in doubt stay a considerate distance away.

Usually, we react to the more subtle signs of annoyance backing away from the whales before we need reminding. Resting whales are often intolerant. If at all possible, we follow at a distance until their behavior changes and close approach is accepted. By learning to recognize the behaviors of the whales and the times when they are particularly sensitive to noise or disturbance, we have become more sensitive in our research activities. Although our group is permitted to approach the whales closely to obtain identification photographs, risking harassment is seldom necessary and generally not desirable.

Though it is sometimes obvious when killer whales are disturbed by the approach of a vessel, the subtle signs of annoyance may escape the notice of the casual observer. Maintaining a proper distance from the whales (100 yards) is the safest course. From this vantage point, observers are much more likely to witness natural behaviors. Also moving a substantial distance ahead of the whales, stopping the boat and engine and permitting the whales to pass at their discretion can be a rewarding experience. Allowing the whales themselves to determine the appropriate boundaries of the interaction is often much more interesting and satisfying than forcing one's presence upon them.

Chapter 8: Killer Whale and Human Interactions

Live-Capture of Killer Whales

It was late in the summer of 1984, and the Prince William Sound salmon purse seine fishery was in full swing. Darkness was falling, and the skipper, his net in the water, could not see the approaching whales. In the fading twilight, the net was closed before the crew realized that the whales were inside. As one crewman leaned over the side to grab a line, a 10,000 pound male killer whale rolled up and exhaled in his face. He fell back in surprise and fright. A second whale blew, and the skipper realized he had a problem. Eventually, after much swearing and stomping on deck, the crew opened the net back up to release the whales which calmly swam out of the net along with about five hundred salmon. Later, someone remarked to the skipper, "Well, you may have lost a thousand dollars worth of fish, but you also let go of about two million dollars worth of whales!" They were referring to the rumored price that Sea World was paying for whales for their oceanarium.

Fortunately, this is the closest any of the killer whales in the Sound has come to actually being captured. On two occasions, in 1977 and 1983, Sea World Inc. announced plans to capture killer whales in Alaska. In 1984, they obtained a federal permit to legally capture killer whales.

The permit stipulated, however, that Sea World must first conduct a population study of killer whales in Alaska. When NGOS was asked to conduct the photoidentification program in Prince William Sound, it created a moral dilemma for our group. On the one hand, we did not wish to appear to be condoning the live-capture of killer whales by participating in the population assessment. On the other hand, a year's full-time research would provide the data needed to decipher the pod structures and make sense of our work from previous years. Here was an opportunity to obtain this much needed information. Our dilemma was one frequently encountered by scientists who strive for objectivity and do not wish to become ensnared in subjective, political battles. Nevertheless, he or she must recognize that decisions regarding funding are more often driven by political considerations than the pursuit of pure knowledge.

Public concern over the projected live-capture began to grow, and the permit was hastily issued before any baseline population study could be completed. We knew that years earlier, photoidentification had demonstrated that the number of killer whales in the inside waters of British Columbia and Puget Sound had been over-estimated. When more accurate population figures became available, public awareness created an outcry which ended the local live-capture of killer whales.

Because no population studies based on photoidentification of Alaska's killer whales existed, Sea World had estimated the population for southern Alaska at three thousand. We suspected this was a serious over-estimation but lacked proof. A population study based on photoidentification could establish a more scientifically justifiable estimate on which the government and public could base management decisions.

An agreement was negotiated with Sea World. Our group would neither publicly support nor oppose the live-capture while research was underway. It was incredibly difficult to keep from being drawn into the controversy. We were scorned by those fighting the live-capture as having been bought off by Sea World. As Alaskans began to unite to oppose the capture, the Sea World front office harangued us for not working to help garner public support for the capture. We were forced to remind them that NGOS was hired to complete a population assessment not to do public relations.

I was joined in the research by Graeme Ellis, Olga von Ziegesar, Kirsten Englund, and Beth Goodwin. To insulate ourselves from the controversy, we chose to remain in the Sound with the whales throughout this period. We survived by blocking out everything but the project at hand. The whales were followed, photographed, recorded, and observed until the pieces of the puzzle began to fit together. The joys of almost daily discoveries made the work exciting. Dorsal fins and killer whale calls haunted our dreams.

By the end of that year, the pods had been sorted out, and we had a good idea of just how many whales were using the Sound. We had photographed 167 killer whales in the Sound and seventy in Southeast Alaska. Although the actual number could be greater, the total of 237 killer whales was probably much closer to the true population than Sea World's unsubstantiated estimate of three thousand. We had also gained a much better understanding of the Sound's killer whales. We discovered that as in British Columbia and Puget Sound, both resident and transient killer whales inhabit the Sound. We made progress in deciphering the local dialects of the resident pods. But most importantly, we established a baseline which would prove invaluable in the future.

When we released the results of our research, opposition to capturing killer whales stiffened in Alaska. There were fewer whales than Sea World had predicted, and it appeared resident whales were organized into stable family groups. Management would have to consider the threat to the social integrity of pods in capturing individual whales. Furthermore, live-capture would probably involve the most frequently seen and most approachable whales. The argument was advanced that these friendly killer whales are a resource that every boating Alaskan could enjoy, and that their existence in the Sound would draw whale watchers and tourists to the state. In the end, the public reaction was clear and strong. The permit to capture whales was revoked.

The question remains whether killer whales should be captured and held in oceanaria. When sizable corporate profits are at stake, the moral issues often become muddied, and the scientific evidence becomes transformed into mere advocacy. Are oceanaria no more than "whale jails" where the inmates are forced to perform in a degrading manner? Or do oceanaria benefit both humanity and whales by increasing public awareness while providing opportunities for research? There is probably truth on both sides. No doubt, oceanaria displays have immeasurably influenced public opinion demonstrating that killer whales are not simply ferocious man-eaters. Spectators are impressed by the sheer size and power of these creatures and by their willingness to work with their human keepers. Undoubtedly, certain research projects such as determining the hearing abilities of killer whales and specific physiological studies have benefited from the availability of captive animals. But having spent many days at oceanaria watching the whales in their daily routines, I have always come away saddened by their obvious neuroses. Captive whales do not resemble those in the wild except in physical form. How can one expect an animal that travels up to ninety miles a day in the wild to react to the limited confines of a cement-walled pool?

Captive breeding has been somewhat successful and offers the possibility of producing killer whales which have known no life outside captivity. It is noteworthy that the most successful captive birthing and rearing program has been in Sea World's five million gallon tank in Florida where the whales have more freedom of movement and privacy from one another. Thus far, captive breeding cannot satisfy the demand for whales at oceanaria. Public opposition to the capture of wild killer whales makes it unlikely that the replacement of the whales currently in captivity will come from this source, especially now that there is a growing awareness of the importance of a stable social structure to the whales' well-being. The future of killer whales in captivity is certainly unclear. In the end, public opinion will decide.

Fig-51. Killer whales expec-
tantly wait for a longline boat
fishing for blackcod to pull its
gear. The killer whales had
learned to remove the fish from
the hooks. Photo by Craig
Matkin.

Killer Whale Fishery Interactions

Killer whales, unlike harbor porpoise and some of the baleen whales, seem to be very "net smart." In years of work in the Sound, I have heard of only one instance of a killer whale's dying as a result of becoming tangled in a net. This happened in a beach lead, a net once used for seining, that was left out all night. To our knowledge, killer whales have never become entangled in any of the light gill nets or heavier purse seine nets currently fished in the Sound. Purse seines encircle and trap salmon, while gillnets entangle the fish. On rare occasions, killer whales may swim into the open circle created by the seine. As in the instance related above, they do not become entangled and usually swim out before the net is closed. Furthermore, resident killer whales usually hunt salmon in the middle of broad passages and ocean entrances away from the shoreline, while seine fishermen work in close to shore. Transient killer whales do patrol shorelines and occasionally encounter fishermen. Once, Lance, Kathy and Eva were following four transients when they entered Long Channel where a seiner's net was stretched almost completely across the narrow passage. There was commotion on board as the whales approached the seine, but to everyone's relief the whales dove and surfaced on the opposite side of the net.

While resident killer whales compete with fishermen for herring and salmon, most fishermen seem to understand and respect the whales as long as they do not interfere directly with their fishing operations. Additionally, fisher-men recognize killer whales as predators of harbor seals and Steller sea lions, which often do take fish from their nets.

Fig-52. This adult male dorsal fin has begun to disintegrate, apparently due to bullet wounding. Photo by Craig Matkin.

Fig-53. In June of 1985, AD34 was photographed with bullet wounds in her dorsal fin. She later died. Photo by C. Matkin.

However, the blackcod longline fishery in Alaska is a different story altogether. In Prince William Sound, the blackcod fishery is a relatively low-budget operation. Most boats are small — less than fifty feet.

Killer whales began interacting with this Prince William Sound fishery in 1985, when a record number of fish were harvested. In April of 1985, I overheard irate fishermen on the VHF radio complaining of raids by killer whales as they pulled in their longlines. At first, we presumed these were isolated and rare occurrences. However, it soon became apparent that the whales had figured out how to obtain a free lunch and were making the most of it.

Fishermen catch blackcod by setting an anchored, mile-long line (groundline) along the ocean floor. Thousands of hooks are attached by short lines at regular intervals along this groundline. Since blackcod inhabit deep water, lines are set in water depths of eight hundred feet or more. The rich, oily fish are then slowly pulled from the bottom — a process that leaves the fish dangling in the water column for five minutes or more. The whales have plenty of time to pull them from the lines, leaving only damaged or empty hooks and occasionally the lips of the blackcod.

In the Bering Sea, where the Japanese fleet have longlined blackcod for many years, killer whales are not a new problem. Interactions with killer whales had been reported since the 1960s, but the problem intensified in the 1980s as the fishery expanded. The Japanese reported running for miles to new fishing grounds to escape the whales. In the 1980s large American vessels entered the lucrative fishery and also suffered substantial losses to killer whales; some fishermen retaliated with high-powered firearms.

During the summer of 1985 in the Sound, small, white, circular wounds that often passed completely through the dorsal fins began to appear in fins of the whales in AB pod. These bullet wounds suggested that the fishery interaction problem in the Sound was much more serious than anticipated. Surveys of the fishermen in the fall of 1985 confirmed our concerns. Nearly every blackcod fisherman reported some problems with killer whales. When the whales were present, they took nearly every fish. An estimated twenty-five percent of the potential catch had been lost to the whales.

Blackcod seem to be an incredibly attractive food for killer whales, probably because, like salmon, they have a very high oil content easily converted to blubber. However, blackcod have not been recovered from killer whale stomachs and are probably not a prominent part of their natural diet (see Appendix 1). Killer whales are not thought to be exceptionally deep divers. U.S. Navy experiments with captive killer whales taught to retrieve objects from the ocean floor suggested they seldom dive deeper than 850 feet. Blackcod, on the other hand, are typically brought to the surface from depths of over 1400 feet. Thus, longline fishermen provide a great service to the whales who wait closer to the surface where they deftly yank the cod from the hooks.

The whales take nearly every blackcod and incidentally caught halibut from the hooks leaving the lower-valued gray cod, turbot, and red snapper. Oftentimes the stout, two inch long hooks are straightened out or broken off, testimony to the force the whales use in grabbing the fish. The only blackcod and halibut left are hooked near tangles in the line. For some reason the whales are reluctant to get near these tangles.

In 1986, the Sea Grant Marine Advisory Program and National Marine Mammal Laboratory both became interested in the fishery interaction problem and helped fund research to answer some of our initial questions. How many fish were being taken? Were the whales being harmed? How did the whales locate the blackcod so effectively? What cues allowed the whales to identify boats fishing for blackcod? Rick Steiner of the Alaska Sea Grant Marine Advisory Program and I began continuous monitoring of the whales while maintaining

Fig-54. Hooked blackcod often are completely removed from longlines. Occasionally, killer whales leave evidence of their work such as these whale bitten fish and the damaged fishing gear. Photo by Craig Matkin.

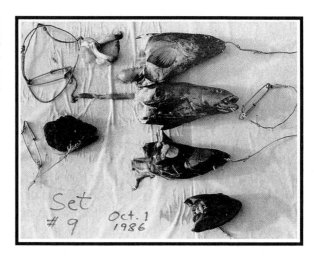

radio contact with the fishing boats. The fishermen reported their location and activities, and we would provided them information on the whales' location and activities. With the aid of fishermen such as Jeff and Jim Aguilar, Harold Kalve, and others who allowed us to observe them and who constantly reported whale sightings, we learned a lot in a short period of time. These fishermen became quite proficient at identifying individual whales and observing their behavior.

It was shocking to watch the whales' activities first-hand. As the fishermen began pulling their longlines, all eyes were on the horizon. Small, splashes in the distance soon became an impressive line of thirty-five killer whales porpoising at high speed toward the fishing gear. It was as if someone had rung the dinner bell. The whales were acutely tuned into the fishing activities. It appeared that only AB pod, a group of thirty-five whales, and possibly closely associated AI pod, with six whales, were involved in the depredations. The females, sometimes with calves alongside, seemed to lead the charge.

Often, the whales did not respond when the fishermen first began pulling their gear. Not until the anchor at the end of the buoy line came off the bottom and the hooked fish dangled in the water column did the whales swim rapidly toward the boat. They would come from up to seven miles away.

We hypothesized that the whales could be keying on the low frequency sounds of the struggling fish, or perhaps on noises made by the longline. Other possibilities were the sound of the boats themselves or the sound of the hydraulics used to pull in the line. This was a surprising discovery since we had not thought that killer whale hearing would be so sensitive to low frequency sounds. Tests of the lower frequency limits to killer whale hearing have been inconclusive because of the high ambient noise levels in the tanks where tests are conducted. Dr. David Bain, however, has established that the upper limit of their hearing is around 105 khz. (compared to 20 khz for humans.) Low frequency sounds travel much greater distances underwater than high frequency sounds. If low frequency sounds were the cue, it meant that the dinner bell could be heard from farther away.

Our goals were to reduce or eliminate killer whale depredations on the blackcod catch and to save the whales from being injured or killed. We identified three possible approaches: to outsmart the whales with a different fishing method; to modify the killer whale's behavior; or, to recommend new equipment. If the whales were keying in on sounds made by the fish themselves, the options were more limited.

To test whether the whales could tell which lines had fish, we conducted an experiment. We instructed one boat to set a longline with unbaited hooks so that no fish would be caught when the gear was pulled. The whales did not respond. The fishermen were disappointed as they had hoped the unbaited line would decoy the whales away from the other boats. Apparently, the whales could tell from a distance which lines had fish on them.

Next, two boats, separated by several miles, tried working together to frustrate the whales. First, one boat pulled its line until the whales got close and then dropped it to the bottom before the whales could remove any fish. Then the other boat pulled its line until the whales got close and again dropped its line before they could get the fish. For a while, the whales charged back and forth over across the miles between the boats, getting no fish. Eventually, the whales milled for a bit then split into two groups; one group went to each boat! At this point, our respect for the intelligence of the killer whale rose a notch or two. Rick shook his head in amazement, and we both realized that fooling these whales would be no simple task.

We began to look at methods to modify their behavior. Steiner developed a number of potential ways for discouraging them. We set our own longlines from the F.V. *Valiant Maid* and attracted the whales to us in order to test his ideas. The Department of Fish and Game permitted us to sell fish that we caught to defray the cost of the research.

Initially, we tried a number of harmless repellents, including an acoustic harassment device developed by Charles Greenlaw and Bruce Mate at Oregon State University. This device, designed to keep harbor seals from eating salmon in front of fish hatcheries, emits strong pulsed sounds at random intervals and frequencies. For a brief time, it seemed to confuse and upset the whales. When the device was first deployed, the whales actually left the area during the pulling of a longline. We were stunned by this unprecedented behavior, but the celebration was short-lived. During the second trial a day later, they seemed to become accustomed to the device and began to completely ignore it.

A second experiment relied on our observation that the whales tended to leave black cod near tangles in the line. Wires that imitated tangles were applied to the lines but with no reduction in losses

We next tried a "bang pipe" — a bell shaped device to which a long hollow pipe is attached. This is plunged into the water and beaten. The Japanese use it for driving porpoise away from their nets. Unfortunately, it only aroused the whale's curiosity, causing them to approach and investigate the device rather than to avoid it. In fact, nearly all the techniques used to confuse or repel the whales aroused only mild curiosity. The raids continued.

Researchers from Hubbs Sea World Research Institute who were also studying the problem believed that the whales might be cueing on changes in the sound of the boat's hydraulic equipment when the lines were pulled. They are currently attempting to silence the hydraulic systems on several vessels. At this point, the evidence is inconclusive. It is conceivable that the killer whales use a number of acoustic clues in locating productive longlines.

The 1985 shootings probably accounted for the disappearance of a number of AB pod whales which had bullet wounds. In all, six whales were lost from the pod during 1985 and 1986 — a mortality rate of about 9%, almost five times the normal rate. Apparently, the bullet wounds did not kill the animals immediately, but long term infections, lead poisoning, or other problems associated with the wounds did. However, the deaths seemed to do little to diminish the whales' desire for blackcod.

Since the killer whale is a long-lived animal with a low reproductive rate, unnatural mortalities may have long term deleterious effects on a pod, on the local population and subsequently on the whale watching tourism industry. Apparently more curious and fearless than most, the AB pod was the most friendly and frequently sighted pod in Prince William Sound, as well as the most daring in stealing fish. Recreational boaters and commercial tourist boats had come to rely on regular sightings of this friendly pod. Commercial fishermen, while protecting their catch, were damaging whales important to the livelihood of others.

Fishermen soon realized that bullets neither stopped nor deterred the whale attacks. Many had never shot at the whales and accepted the activities of the whales as a frustrating but inevitable problem. Even those that did use guns had no strong desire to harm the whales, but the frustration ran so strong that their initial reaction was to shoot at them. Some fishermen developed increasing respect for the whales as they learned to recognize individuals and realized that these pods were comprised of family groups that had been in the Sound for many years. Furthermore, shooting at the whales was beginning to stir up a public outcry which could only hurt the fishermen in the long run. Unlike the "wild west" scenario occurring in the Bering Sea, Prince William Sound was a highly visible area where the fishermen's actions did not go unnoticed. The fishery in the Sound involves a relatively small group of involved local people who had no desire to destroy their fishery or the whales. In 1986, the Marine Mammal Protection Act was revised to make it illegal to shoot whales, even if they were stealing a fisherman's catch. After 1986, we observed no new bullet wounds.

Since 1986, fishermen have sought other solutions to the problem. A trick that sometimes worked was a variation on our first experiment. Fishermen placed their longlines in widely separated areas. If the whales approached when pulling one set of gear, the gear was dropped, and the boat moved to another string of gear in another area miles away. This was not an efficient way to fish and was not always effective at discouraging the whales, but it was better than losing the entire catch.

A few fishermen experimented with the use of explosives in an attempt to scare the whales before they got near the lines. Charges were set when the whales were first seen and before they began preying on the hooked fish. For a few seasons, this seemed to reduce losses for the handful of fishermen willing to work with high explosives. A charge of plastic explosive equal to a couple sticks of dynamite was required to dissuade the whales. The use of explosives was not universally condoned for fear that even at a distance it might damage the whale's sensitive acoustic systems, but no other solution had been found. Regular observations of AB pod in 1987 and 1988 indicated a mortality rate of about three percent, and the whales seemed to feed and behave normally. In 1988, fishermen reported that explosives were no longer effective. Their use was being abandoned. The use of explosives was potentially illegal (if whales were killed or injured) and was basically dangerous for both fishermen and whales.

In the meantime, AB pod continued frequently to approach vessels. In 1988, five calves were born into the pod, which we hoped signaled a recovery from the mortalities of previous years.

In 1989, the blackcod fishery was closed because of concerns that the fish might come into contact with oil from the *Exxon Valdez*. When fishing resumed in 1990, depredations appeared to be somewhat reduced.

In 1991, the blackcod season was delayed until May 15. By this time, some salmon were already returning to the Sound. There were no problems with whales in the first two weeks of the season and only sporadic depredations in early June. The presence of salmon may distract the whales enough to substantially reduce killer whale interactions with the fishery. It may make sense to delay the opening of the Prince William Sound blackcod fishery until mid-June when more salmon are present, and AB pod may be elsewhere.

In 1992, the blackcod season in the Sound was reduced to about two weeks, because the large number of fishing vessels quickly caught their quota. Although killer whales did raid longlines, because of the short season, the fishery-wide losses were reduced. In 1993 even more boats participated in the fishery, but the season was opened only four days, so the killer whale problem was negligible.

Shorter and later fishing seasons may reduce the amount of interaction between whales and fishermen, but elimination of the problem might require a change in fishing gear. In Canada, where pots or traps are used exclusively to fish for blackcod, there is no problem despite an abundance of killer whales. Unfortunately, such a change in Alaska would be costly for fishermen and involve confrontations with longline fishermen's associations. In the long run, however, it is probably the most practical solution.

In recent years (1991-1993), there is some suspicion that pods other than AB pod may have picked up the fish stealing habit. In the winter, killer whales have been taking fish from the gray cod longlines set in and near the Sound. Although the whales do not take the gray cod, they remove all the incidentally caught halibut and blackcod which the fishermen are not allowed to keep at that time of year. These depredations may not cost the fishermen much financially, but they do try their patience.

Problems between fishermen and killer whales are far worse in the western Gulf of Alaska and Bering Sea and could have a far greater impact on killer whale populations. In these blackcod fisheries, which are much larger and more lucrative than the Sound's, shootings are commonplace. Recently, they have been verified in photographs taken by the National Marine Mammal Laboratory. One fisherman described the situation as "all-out war." In 1991, National Marine Fisheries Service observers documented the deaths of several killer whales.

As man alters the marine ecosystem, overall effects must be considered. The substantial human extraction of fish from the oceans is a less obvious human impact on the whales. Many fish stocks that we exploit such as herring, salmon, cod, halibut, and turbot are also important to killer whales. We know little of the winter feeding ecology of killer whales. If the whales depend on bottomfish, our exploitation of these resources may eventually have an impact on the whales. However, improved management of native salmon stocks and establishment of fish hatcheries may provide increased or more consistent salmon runs thus benefiting the whales.

Killer Whales and the *Exxon Valdez* Oil Spill

I was working in the bilge of the dry-docked *F.V. Lucky Star* in Seward, Alaska on the morning of March 24, 1989, when I flipped on the radio to catch the news. The newscast began —"Perhaps one of the greatest ecological disasters in history occurred this morning in what may become this countries largest oil spill . . . ." Where could this have happened, I pondered as I worked— the Gulf of Mexico? The announcer continued: "In Prince William Sound, Alaska, the *Exxon Valdez* has run aground on Bligh Reef spilling at least eight million gallons of crude oil." The words stunned me. There had to be some mistake! This news stirred in me a similar shock, disbelief, and anger that the announcement of the attack on Pearl Harbor must have aroused in my parents. I ran to call Rick Steiner in Cordova. Sounding numb, he had just returned from a small plane flight over the bleeding tanker. He spoke of sea lions and birds swimming at the periphery of the spill and no effort being made to contain the oil. It was time to prepare my boat and family and head for the Sound.

Since March 24, 1989 nothing has been the same, nor will it be the same in the foreseeable future, if ever. I speak not only from an ecological but also from a social and personal perspective. The spill and its gruesome aftermath have changed our way of looking at life in Alaska. Suddenly, Alaska does not seem quite so remote and immune from the ecological disasters that haunt most of the rest of the world today. It is more than clear that no unspoiled wilderness, no wild country is safe, unless we take a more active role in insuring its safety.

In a couple days, the *Lucky Star* was ready for service and I was joined by Olga and our year old daughter. We headed for the Sound to join other volunteers. The rivers of oil had not yet reached the southwestern corner of the Sound and the Port San Juan Fish Hatchery; so the first priority for the volunteer fleet was to boom off the hatchery and protect the young fish. For a couple days, we unloaded helicopters and strung together oil booms. More and more fishing boats arrived daily.

We were hopeful that the killer whales had left the Sound in front of the spreading slick. There was some debate as to whether whales and porpoises avoided oil slicks. We hoped they would. One unconfirmed report placed a small group of killer whales near the tanker. Then, we received a radio call from the Alaska Department of Fish and Game. At least thirty killer whales had been sighted from an airplane in the area south of Knight Island. Anxiously, we headed out to find them.

The oil now was just coming down along Point Helen at the south end of Knight Island. Thick and sticky, the crude splashed up on the *Lucky Star*, creating a black bow wave that clung to the sides of our boat. The petroleum vapors caught in our throats. This was it; the first smelly crude, pushed by wind and currents, was charging into the pristine waters of the southwestern Sound. Millions of gallons were soon to follow. High winds a couple of days after the spill had churned much of the oil into a thick "mousse" — an incredibly sticky oil and water emulsion that forms thick blankets on the water and beaches. In some places, the mousse was nearly a foot thick on the surface. The thought of a whale trying to breathe as it surfaced through the mousse was horrifying.

We finally encountered the whales in oil free waters south of Knight Island. That day was spent traveling back and forth with the whales as they circled in a dispersed formation. We took many pictures of the whales and discovered that seven of the thirty-six AB pod whales photographed the previous September were not present. This was March 31, only six days after the spill. Graeme Ellis, in his initial examination of the photographs, could not believe we had photographed the entire pod. Months later, subsequent encounters confirmed our fears. Nearly twenty percent of the pod seemed to have vanished. The fact that missing whales included mothers leaving orphaned calves and that many of the missing whales were juveniles aroused our suspicion that the probable cause was the oil spill. Furthermore, whales were missing from many of the maternal (family) groups that make up the pod. Seldom do any whales other than older, post reproductive animals die from natural causes. As the sunlight faded at the end of the day, we watched with dismay as the whales headed up Knight Island Passage and through the sheen of oil slicks. AB pod was not photographed again in the Sound until late that summer.

It was extremely fortunate that our research group had the support of private donors and the state of Alaska in the years immediately prior to the spill.

Without the photoidentification data for those years, it would not have been possible to recognize the immediate effects of this disaster. Many agencies were caught flatfooted without the "baseline" information needed to measure the effects of the oil on various other species. Indeed, no one took the possibility of the spill seriously until it actually happened. The lesson is: wherever there is tanker traffic, there will eventually be some kind of spill; therefore, preventative measures and basic monitoring of natural systems should be mandatory.

Since 1989, the pods of killer whales have been carefully observed and meticulously photographed. With the support of the National Marine Mammal Laboratory in Seattle, NGOS continued the assessment of the killer whale population in the Sound for the next three years. Thus far, the most striking changes have been within AB pod — once our major resident pod. In fact, this is the only resident pod in the Sound that has shown reduced numbers since the spill. In the year following the spill, another six whales were lost raising the total to thirteen. There was one more death and a single birth in 1991. The number of whales in the pod had declined from thirty-six in 1988 to twenty-three in 1990.

Many of the friendly whales I have described above (including AB8 "Bubbles") were lost following the spill. AB8 left a young calf, AB41, who surprisingly has been "adopted" by other whales in the pod and continues to survive in 1993. Another orphaned calf, AB38, also survives. It was in poor condition in 1992 but frisky and friendly in 1993.

The large, adult males AB2 (see Fig-23) and AB3 (see Figs-56-57) both had their fins begin collapsing after the spill. This may indicate poor condition. In 1991, federal funding for this work ended, but private funding has kept the monitoring program alive.

The following diagram illustrates the relationships within AB pod. Some of the maternal groups are quite tentative, because the whales died before they could be placed with confidence. The diagram clearly shows how some of these groups were affected, first by interactions with fishermen and then by the devastating *Exxon Valdez* oil spill.

The loss of so many young females and juveniles from AB pod raises a question of whether the pod will be able to rebuild itself. It is difficult to assess the importance of the missing whales to the pod's social structures. Will there be difficulties in raising young with so many missing adult females? Will the whales in some of the devastated maternal groups lose their connection with the pod? Since mortalities on this scale have never been previously documented, the outcome is unpredictable.

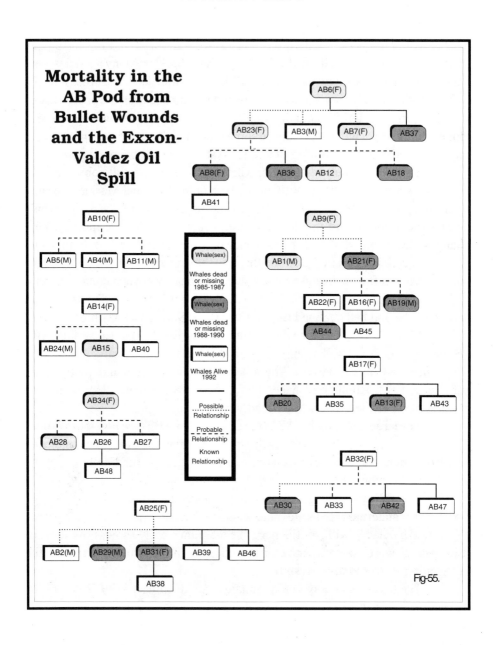

Mortality in the AB Pod from Bullet Wounds and the Exxon-Valdez Oil Spill

Fig-55.

Fig-56. A3, a mature male, was photographed during the 1984 baseline survey. Photo by Craig Matkin.

Fig-57. AB3's dorsal fin folded over at the time of the spill. By 1991, the collapse was complete. Photo by Eva Saulitis.

In 1990, AB pod was seldom seen traveling as a single unit. AB pod whales often began to appear on the periphery of multipod aggregations and seemed to be more timid than in the past. No new calves were born into the pod. In 1991, the pod was infrequently encountered, and we wondered if they were avoiding the Sound. However, in 1991 the first calf since the spill was born. During the 1992 and 1993 seasons, some encouraging signs of recovery began to appear. AB pod began to travel as a cohesive unit. Two new calves were born in 1992, and another was born in 1993. For the first time since the spill, there were no mortalities. One of the new calves of 1992, AB47, was born in midsummer, a very unusual event. Eva Saulitis first spotted it when it was less than a day old, a tiny, orange-tinged, whale swimming close by the side of its mother, AB 32. She had lost her calf, AB42, following the spill.

In 1992, AB pod was once again the most frequently sighted pod in the Sound. As we photographed them, we noted that some of the young whales were quite friendly and frequently approached the skiff. Interestingly, AB41, the orphan daughter of AB8 was the friendliest of the young whales, and often rode in the stern wake of the skiff just like her mother, Bubbles, had done in the past.

Thus, we have hopes for eventual recovery of this battered pod. Long-term study will allow us to chart the pod's future and should provide additional understanding of the social workings within resident killer whale pods. This will give us a better idea of the social effects caused by the sudden removal of a number of whales from a pod — information which may be of use in evaluating the effects of live-capture.

Since the bodies of the thirteen AB pod whales were not recovered, we will never know the precise cause of their deaths. Although some would like to blame these deaths on interaction with the longline fishery, this is unlikely. There had been no signs of bullet wounds for several years prior to the spill, and the blackcod fishery had not been open since the spring of 1988. In September of 1988, all the whales in AB pod had been accounted for, and nothing abnormal was noticed. If disease or another natural disaster were responsible, it seems highly unlikely that only the AB pod would have been affected. The coincidence of the oil spill and unprecedented mortality rates are evidence too compelling to ignore. The oil spill provides the most plausible explanation for the decline of the AB pod.

I suspect that AB pod was in the path of the uncontrolled spread of the oil that occurred during the high winds of March 27. It is plausible that inhalation of the thickened mouse or the toxic vapors could have caused the death of the initial seven whales. The others died later, perhaps from respiratory complica-

Fig-58. AB32, who lost her calf during the spill, gave birth on July 25, 1992 to his calf, AB47, who was a day old when first photographed. This is the only summer birth we have ever recorded. Photo by Eva Saulitis.

tions or other chronic effects of petroleum inhalation. Mammals inhaling oil or heavy hydrocarbon vapors may suffer lung damage which may eventually lead to respiratory failure from pneumonia. Even small amounts can have serious effects. Inhalation of hydrocarbons seems to be far more immediately dangerous for whales than ingestion or skin contact.

When killer whales breathe, they begin exhalation before reaching the surface where they inhale. The gruesome possibility exists that members of AB pod emerged into the thick, gooey layers of wind-whipped mousse and inhaled the toxic material. The patchiness of the wind driven slick may have exposed certain pod members while sparing others. Resident killer whales frequently travel in widespread formation. It is also conceivable that constant and repeated inhalation of the abundant toxic fumes present immediately following the spill was lethal to some whales.

A number of whales in the AT1 group of transients have not been photographed since just before or shortly after the spill. A group of four AT1 whales which often traveled together (AT5, AT6, AT7, AT8) were photographed near the *Exxon Valdez* in the early days of the spill. All but one (AT6) has been missing since 1989. Because transient whales are seen less consistently from year to year than residents, it is not certain that the missing whales are dead. However, nine of the twenty-one members of the AT1 group have not been photographed since 1989, and we suspect that at least some of these may be dead. One group member, AT19, has been identified washed up dead on a beach. Two

Fig-59. A killer whale exhaling before breaking the surface of the water. It is possible that killer whales inhaled crude oil or hydrocarbon vapors that damaged their lungs leading to respiratory failure. Photo by Craig Matkin.

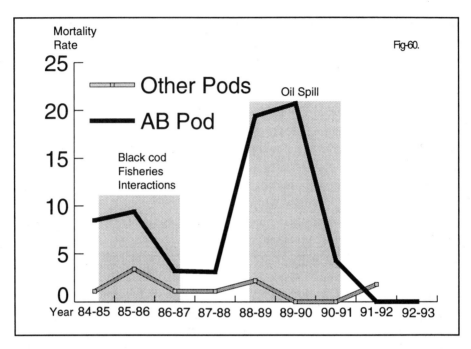

Fig-60.

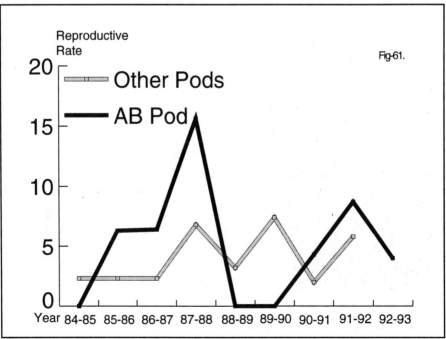

Fig-61.

other dead killer whales, too decomposed to identify, were also found on beaches in 1990. One of these contained marine mammal parts indicating that it was a transient. Before that year, we had never seen a dead killer whale on a beach in the Sound as generally, killer whales sink when they die. Since 1990, two additional unidentifiable killer whales have been found on beaches within or adjacent to the Sound, bringing the total of dead, beached whales to five since 1989. Stomachs of both of these whales contained marine mammal parts.

It may take years of observation before the ultimate effects of the spill become apparent. Long-term effects on the food chain may still be occurring and may be difficult to evaluate. For example, transient whales may have accumulated toxins after ingesting the lethargic, oil-soaked harbor seals that were left in the wake of the oil. Reproductive failure due to hydrocarbon accumulation has been observed in some mammals. Also, following the spill there has been a sharp reduction in the number of harbor seals in the western Sound, which may have an effect on the transient killer whales that depend upon them for sustenance.

A Successful Day with the Whales

Many days in the field are little more than waiting for the wind to stop howling and the rain to end its deluge. On many calm, clear days, the whales are neither seen nor heard; days may pass without finding whales. At other times, we have listened for hours on the hydrophone with growing frustration as whales swam nearby through impenetrable fog. But on occasion, fortune smiles on us; the combination of good weather and the presence of whales makes the all effort and patience worthwhile.

It is the third of September, 1992, and Dr. John Ford, Graeme Ellis and I are assessing the composition of various resident pods in southwestern Prince William Sound. Dr. Ford is also attempting to collect recordings of single pods, aiding us in our continuing efforts to define the dialects of resident whales. It is about 6:45 in the morning when we roll out of the bunks, plunk the hydrophone into the water, and prepare the morning coffee or tea. The weather has been good, so the *Lucky Star* is anchored in Sleepy Bay. This open and exposed bay offers a view of Lower Knight Island Passage and Montague Strait; but more important, it provides an unobstructed acoustic avenue for monitoring the area. For the first hour of the morning, we listen for killer whale calls and talk over the day's agenda. All plans are provisional for as soon as the whales are found, their activities determine our activities.

Our fortunes are good this morning. John's sensitive ear soon recognizes the faint and intermittent calls of killer whales on the hydrophone — a far more potent stimulant to this crew than the muddy coffee we are drinking. There is a brief discussion as to the identity of the whales from the calls. It appears that both AB and AI pods may be some miles away. Scanning from the crows nest, twenty-five feet above the deck, I am unable to locate the whales. We lower the directional hydrophone and determine the approximate direction of the vocalizations. The calls become stronger as John pulls up the hydrophone; Graeme raises the anchor, and the *Lucky Star* steams out of the bay towing our twenty-one foot skiff behind.

After traveling about twenty minutes and scanning constantly with binoculars, we stop to listen again on the directional hydrophone. The whales are close now. We spot them: it is the six whales of AI pod. John moves the *Lucky Star* several hundred yards ahead of the whales, shuts down the engine and begins to record and scribble notes. Because this is a single pod, he can be assured of recording calls only specific to this single pod. As Graeme and I pull away in the skiff, we leave John animated, jotting notes on pod calls and commenting on their nuances. In the skiff we quickly take identification photographs, trying not to let the sound of our motor interfere with John's recordings. The six whales are spread out over several hundred yards. Occasionally, one chases a salmon. Quickly, I snap identification photographs. Each whale is identified visually and checked off as we go. First there is AI2, an adult male, then AI5 and AI6, two maturing males so similar in appearance and age that we suspect they are twins. Across the way is AI4, a young female born in 1984, and her mother, AI3.

A call from John on the VHF radio interrupts our activities. He is now hearing faint calls from another pod. "Sounds like AB pod is headed this way," he informs us. About fifteen minutes later, we see the first AB pod whales. Once again, calls identify the pod long before we can see it. Suddenly, we are surrounded by juvenile whales. AB38 and AB40 appear rambunctious as they dash under the skiff. AB41, orphan of AB8 (Bubbles), is soon riding our stern wake. We are as excited as the whales since the playing juveniles offer a great chance to determine their sexes. If they turn belly up, as they sometimes do in play, a glimpse may be had of their genital area. Keeping each calf's identity straight is not always easy; they are exceptionally quick and mix in intricate swimming patterns. Good fortune is with us, and we are able to determine the sex of three whales: AB38, AB40 and AB41.

Fig-62. As killer whale calves play in the exuberance of their youth, researchers have an opportunity to determine their sex. Photo by Graeme Ellis.

Instantly, AB38 and AB40, charge off toward an adult which appears to be chasing salmon. We arrive in time to see a flash of silver in the mouth of a whale. "Grab the scale net," Graeme shouts as I scramble to the side of the skiff. The flickering of salmon scales drifting down to the depths is interrupted by the swish of the fine mesh net. "Got a few," I report, sliding the scales into a small envelope. These scale samples will confirm the kill and allow positive identification of the prey species.

Just behind us, the two juveniles are chasing another salmon. This fish swims right beneath the boat and so do the whales. One whale erupts from the water near the bow of the boat, and I see a flash of silver. I swing the net in the water and come up with more than scales — egg skeins and fish entrails with flesh attached cling to the mesh. One of the young whales suddenly appears. I get a look that tells me sampling their lunch is not appreciated. Quickly, I pop the morsel back in the water, retaining a couple of scales.

As we drift and watch, individual whales spread out across the Strait, twist, turn and swim tight circles pursuing the salmon. This is a poor time for photoidentification, so we return to the *Lucky Star* for lunch, hoping the feeding whales will again coalesce into groups. In the afternoon, the whales head north and begin to swim in their maternal groups. Speeding from group to group, Graeme drives the skiff and checks off each individual as I photograph with the motor driven, autofocus camera. This routine is practically automatic for both of us after having worked together for the past decade. Smoothly, we move in to snap pictures, then slide away, paralleling the course of the whales, keeping mental note of the whales that have been photographed.

The seas begin to build as the wind picks up in late afternoon. The whales are entering a group resting mode, moving slowly in tight formation, the spray cascading over their snouts as they rise to breathe. When group resting, the whales resent being disturbed so we angle away, glad to obtain shelter from wind and spray for ourselves and our equipment. The skiff is quickly secured for towing, the equipment off-loaded, and the *Lucky Star* makes way for protected waters.

It has been a successful day. We have determined the sexes of three young whales, collected five salmon scale samples and confirmed the identities of the mothers of three new calves in AB pod. In addition, John has made some valuable recordings. The excitement of another glimpse into the lives of the whales fades slowly. Speculation and discussion based on the day's observations lasts well into the evening.

Future Research

Not all questions concerning scientific research are amenable to resolution by simply applying the scientific method. Questions of value are also important. For example, does the knowledge gained by studying killer whales in captivity justify the shorter life span and discomfort experienced by the whales? If the knowledge gained ultimately insures their survival in the wild, then is their captivity justified? New research methods to study killer whales in the wild raise similar questions.

In our study of Prince William Sound's whales, we have chosen photoidentification and acoustic monitoring as these research techniques are both effective and unintrusive. However, as with all techniques, they possess inherent built-in limitations.

New techniques, such as genetic analysis, have the potential to prove decisively whether observed differences between resident and transient whales are genetically based or are merely behavioral. Secondly, if the AT1 group of transients proves to be genetically isolated from other transients (as well as the residents), then their decrease in numbers since the spill may have created an endangered population. Similarly, genetic studies might be able to determine just how genetically distinct AB pod is from other resident pods. Genetic analysis would also help us to understand kinship structures both within pods and between pods. For example, we might be able to determine decisively whether a smaller pod found in association with a larger pod is a splinter pod. Furthermore, we might be able to understand how resident whales with their close knit and life-long pod structures interbreed with other pods, avoiding genetic stagnation. Genetic clarification of relationships within a pod's social structure could provide invaluable information for management decisions such as the amount of social disruption caused by capture for live displays. However, genetic study requires direct disturbance of the wild whales to obtain a small scrape of skin. Does the knowledge gained justify any disruption, pain, or fright caused the animals in obtaining these samples?

A small sample of tissue would also be helpful in assessing the exposure of whales to certain man-made pollutants, such as PCBs, dioxin, heavy metals, aromatic hydrocarbons, and pesticides. Systematic monitoring of these contaminants would require tissue sampling from live, wild whales. Samples from some killer whales found stranded in Alaska, Washington State, and British Columbia have shown high contaminant levels of DDT and PCB. Environmental monitoring by analysis of small amounts of tissue from a top predator such as the killer whale may provide a good measure of general pollution levels in the ocean. This monitoring might warn of dangers not only to killer whales but to other species as well. Once again, one is confronted with the question of whether the end justifies the means in pursuing these questions.

Before projects involving large-scale tissue sampling proceed, the effect of biopsies on the whales must be examined. Canadian researchers are taking the lead, recording and examining the behavior of whales after such samples have been taken. Initial observations indicate little reaction to these disturbances. However, researchers are proceeding cautiously. Any serious disturbance of the whales would be untenable. Changes in the whale's behavior around boats would have long-term consequences and could disrupt our long-term photoidentification studies which are essential in providing a framework for all other research. Thus far, the whales have been approachable even immediately after taking the tissue sample.

A second frontier in whale research is the potential for tracking whales by satellite. But once again, this requires that we disturb them by attaching radio transmitters. Technological advances provide ever smaller radio transmitters capable of relaying the positions of a whale continuously, measuring the time the whale spends beneath the surface, the depth of the its dives, and the water temperature. Details on the whale's movements may yield clues as to their ranges and winter feeding habits. However, killer whales did not tolerate the larger radio tags applied to them in Puget Sound some years ago. Adequate methods for attaching transmitters without having to capture the whales have not yet been developed. Once again, the question remains — is disturbance of the whales worth the potential return of information?

All new forms of research need not be intrusive, however. For example, acoustic monitoring of the whales from remote hydrophones attached to buoys scattered throughout their range could yield valuable information on their year round distribution and movements. Such studies would be able to determine which areas are important to the survival of the whales. Because each pod has distinct calls, a pod's identity could be determined from these recordings. Thus, we could discover not only which whales were in an area but their numbers as we have data on the sizes of the various pods. All this would be available from remote transmitting stations which would relay the information directly to the lab. This project would require some maintenance but would be considerably less expensive than satellite monitoring.

Regardless of how one resolves the question of whether to pursue more intrusive kinds of research, it is most important that photoidentification and acoustic studies continue. The information provided by careful photoidentification studies will continue to enlighten scientists and the public as to the uniqueness of this species and the need for its protection. In addition, observations from these efforts will provide decision-makers with long-term baseline data crucial for monitoring the health of the marine environment and insuring the future survival of the killer whale.

Appendix 1. Inventory of Alaska species preyed upon by killer whales, from evidence reported for locations in Alaska and British Columbia.

Prey	Evidence	Location	Source
Toothed Whales, Dolphins, and Porpoises			
Dall's porpoise	kill seen	Prince William S.	Hall *et al.* 1985
Phocoenoides dalli	attacks	Prince William S.	Saulitis 1993
	attack	Southeast Alaska	Barr and Barr 1972
	attack	Southeast Alaska	D'Vincent *et al.* 1989
	attacks	Southeast Alaska	Jefferson *et al.* 1991
	attacks	British Columbia	Pike and MacAskie 1969
	attack	British Columbia	Jacobson 1986
	stomach	British Columbia	Bigg, Ellis, *et al.* 1990
	attack	British Columbia	Morton 1990
	attack	British Columbia	Jefferson *et al.* 1991
	attack	British Columbia	R. W. Baird, pers. com.
Harbor porpoise	kill seen	Prince William S.	Hall *et al.* 1985
Phocoena phocoena	kill	Prince William S.	K. Heise, pers. com.
	stomach	Cape St. Elias	K. Wynne, pers. com.
	stomach	British Columbia	Ford and Ford 1981
	stomach	British Columbia	Bigg, Ellis, *et al.* 1990
	seen feeding	British Columbia	Morton 1990
	kill	British Columbia	R. W. Baird, pers. com.
Pacific white-sided dolphin	attack	Southeast Alaska	M. E. Dahlheim, pers. com.
Legenorhynchus obliquidens	attack	Southeast Alaska	Hastings 1993
Beluga	seen feeding	Arctic	Scammon 1874
Delphinapterus leucas	kill reported	Point Lay	Frost *et al.* 1983
	kill reported	Point Hope	Frost *et al.* 1983
	kill seen	Kivalina	Frost *et al.* 1983
	attack	Kotzebue Sound	Burns and Seaman 1986
	kill reported	Kotzebue Sound	Burns and Seaman 1986
	kills seen	Bering Sea	Tomilin 1957
	carcass	St. Lawrence Island	Frost *et al.* 1983
	attack	S.E. Bering Sea	Frost *et al.* 1992
	seen feeding	Kuskokwim Bay	Frost *et al.* 1992
	kills seen	Bristol Bay	King 1989
	attack	Bristol Bay	Frost *et al.* 1992
	stomach	Turnagain Arm	D. Bain, pers. commun.
Baleen Whales			
Humpback whale	attack	Southern Alaska	Lockley 1979
Megaptera novaeangliae	attack	Prince William S.	N. Naslund, pers. com.
	attack	Southeast Alaska	D. McSweeney, pers.
	attack	Southeast Alaska	D'Vincent *et al.* 1989
	harassment	Southeast Alaska	Jefferson *et al.* 1991
Gray whale	kill reported	Beaufort Sea	Frost *et al.* 1983
Eschrichtius robustus	attack	Point Hope	Marquette 1978
	attacks	Bering Strait	Lowry *et al.* 1987

	stomach	Bering Sea	Zenkovich 1938
	carcass	Bering Sea	Fay *et al.* 1979
	attack	Bering Sea	Ivashin and Votrogov 1982
	attack	St. Lawrence Island	Ljungblad and Moore 1983
	attack	British Columbia	Pike and MacAskie 1969
Minke whale	attack	Dutch Harbor	Lowry *et al.* 1987
Balaenoptera	kill reported	Gulf of Alaska	Fiscus *et al.* 1976
acutorostrata	kill seen	Gulf of Alaska	Anonymous 1977
	attack, kill	Prince William S.	Mehlberg 1986
	attack	Yakutat	Hall 1986
	carcass	British Columbia	Ford and Ford 1981
	kill seen	British Columbia	Hancock 1965
Right whale	attack	Bering Sea	Tomilin 1957
Eubalaena glacialis	attack reported	British Columbia	Gaskin 1982
Fin whale	bite marks	N.E. Bering Sea	Zenkovich 1938
Balaenoptera physalus	stomach	Bering Sea	Tomilin 1957
	attack	Alaska Peninsula	Murie 1959
	attack	British Columbia	Pike and MacAskie 1969
Bowhead whale	prey scars	Arctic	Tomilin 1957
Balaena mysticetus	kill seen	Barrow	Bailey and Hendee 1926

Pinnipeds and Sea Otter

Bearded seal	stomach	Bering Sea	Zenkovich 1938
Erignathus barbatus			
Northern fur seal	seen feeding	Bering Sea	Tomilin 1957
Callorhinus ursinus	seen feeding	Pribilof Islands	Hanna 1923
	stomach	Pribilof Islands	Hanna 1923
	stomach	Pribilof Islands	Zenkovich 1938
Harbor seal	stomach	Nome	Lowry *et al.* 1987
Phoca vitulina	seen feeding	Bristol Bay	Frost *et al.* 1992
	kills seen	Prince William S.	Hall *et al.* 1985
	kills, attacks	Prince William S.	E. L. Saulitis, unpubl. data
	stomach	Prince William S.	E. L. Saulitis, unpubl. data
	stomach	Cape St. Elias	K. Wynne, pers. com.
	predation	Glacier Bay	Calambokidis *et al.* 1987
	attack	British Columbia	Moran 1924
	attack	British Columbia	Fisher 1952
	stomach	British Columbia	Bigg, Ellis, *et al.* 1990
	kills seen	British Columbia	Heimlich-Boran and Heimlich-Boran 1990
	kills seen	British Columbia	Baird and Stacey 1987, 1988; Baird *et al.* 1990
	seen feeding	British Columbia	Morton 1990
	stomach	British Columbia	Pike and MacAskie 1969
Steller sea lion	attack	Bering Sea	Turner 1886
Eumetopias jubatus	pursuit	Bering Sea	Branson 1971
	attack	N.E. Bering Sea	Zenkovich 1938
	attack	Bristol Bay	G. Sheffield, pers. commun.
	attack	Bristol Bay	Frost *et al.* 1992
	kill seen	Alaska Peninsula	Murie 1959
	attack	Gulf of Alaska	Brueggeman *et al.* 1987
	seen feeding	Prince William S.	Hall 1986

	stomach	Prince William S.	E. L. Saulitis, unpubl. data
	stomach	Cape St. Elias	K. Wynne, pers. commun.
	attack	Southeast Alaska	Dolphin 1987
	attack	Southeast Alaska	D'Vincent *et al.* 1989
	predation	B.C. and Alaska	Scammon 1874
	attacks	British Columbia	Pike and MacAskie 1969
	attack	British Columbia	Harbo 1975
	attack	British Columbia	Hoyt 1984
	attack	British Columbia	Bigg *et al.* 1987
	stomach	British Columbia	Bigg, Ellis, *et al.* 1990
	seen feeding	Central B.C. coast	Morton 1990
	attack	W. Bering Sea	Tomilin 1957
	predation	North Pacific	Mikhalev *et al.* 1981
Northern elephant seal	attack	British Columbia	Stacey and Baird 1989
Mirounga angustirostris	stomach	British Colunbia	Bigg, Ellis, *et al.* 1990
	stomach	British Colunbia	Ford and Ford 1981
Pacific walrus	seen feeding	Bering Strait	Scammon 1874
Odobenus rosmarus	kills reported	Bering Strait	Bailey and Hendee 1926
divergens	carcass	Bering Strait	Lowry *et al.* 1987
	kill seen	Bering Sea	Frost *et al.* 1992
	carcass	St. Lawrence Island	Fay and Kelly 1980
	attack	Cape Peirce	Mazzone 1987
	ramming	Bristol Bay	G. Sheffield, pers. commun.
	kills seen	W. Bering Sea	Tomilin 1957
Sea otter	kill	Southeast Alaska	P. Johnson, pers. commun.
Enhydra lutris			

Terrestrial Mammals

River otter	chase	Prince William S.	E. L. Saulitis, unpubl. data
Lutra canadensis	chase	British Columbia	Morton 1990
Deer	seen feeding	British Columbia	Pike and MacAskie 1969
Odocoileus hemionus sitkensis			
Moose	kill	Southeast Alaska	Kochman 1992
Alces alces			

Fishes

Salmon	seen feeding	Bering Sea	Scammon 1874
Oncorhynchus spp.	seen feeding	Kodiak Island	Leatherwood *et al.* 1983
	scales	Prince William S.	NGOS
	seen feeding	Prince William S.	Hall 1986
	seen feeding	Prince William S.	C. O. Matkin, unpubl. data
	seen feeding	Prince William S.	E. L. Saulitis, unpubl. data
	seen feeding	Pacific Northwest	Bigg *et al.* 1987
	seen feeding	British Columbia	Ford and Ford 1981
	seen feeding	British Columbia	Jacobson 1986
	stomachs	British Columbia	Bigg, Ellis, *et al.* 1990
Steelhead	scales	British Columbia	R. W. Baird, pers. commun.
Oncorhynchus mykiss			
Pacific halibut	stomach	Gulf of Alaska	Fiscus *et al.* 1976
Hippoglossus stenolepis	stomach	Kodiak Island	Rice 1968
	seen feeding*	Prince William S.	H. Kalve, pers. commun.
	stomach	British Columbia	Pike and MacAskie 1969
Capelin	seen feeding	W. Bering Sea	Tomilin 1957
Mallotus villosus			
Atka mackerel	seen feeding	W. Bering Sea	Tomilin 1957
Pleurogrammus monopterygius			

Pacific cod	stomach	W. Bering Sea	Tomilin 1957
Gadus macrocephalus			
Shark	stomach	N.E. Pacific coast	Rice 1968
	stomach	W. Bering Sea	Tomilin 1957
Skate	stomach	W. Bering Sea	Tomilin 1957
Family Rajidae			
Pacific herring	seen feeding	Prince William S.	C. O. Matkin, unpubl. data
Clupea pallasi	seen feeding	British Columbia	Jacobson 1986
	stomach	British Columbia	Bigg, Ellis, *et al.* 1990
	stomach	W. Bering Sea	Tomilin 1957
Sablefish	seen feeding*	Bering Sea	Matkin 1988
Anoplopoma fimbria	reports*	Bering Sea, Gulf of Alaska	Dahlhéim 1988
	seen feeding*	Gulf of Alaska	Matkin *et al.* 1986
	seen feeding*	Prince William S.	Matkin 1986
	seen feeding*	Prince William S.	H. Kalve, pers. commun.
Smelt	stomach	W. Bering Sea	Tomilin 1957
Family Osmeridae			

Mollusks

Squid or octopus beak	stomach	Prince William S.	E. L. Saulitis, unpubl. data

Birds

Black brant	attack	British Columbia	Scheffer and Slipp 1948
Branta bernicla nigricans			
Cormorant	stomach	British Columbia	Ford and Ford 1981
Phalacrocorax sp.			
Pelagic cormorant	chase	British Columbia	R. W. Baird, pers. commun.
Phalacrocorax pelagicus			
Rhinoceros auklet	chase	British Columbia	Stacey and Baird 1989
Cerorhinca monocerata	harassed	British Columbia	Morton 1990
Horned grebe	kill	British Columbia	Stacey and Baird 1989
Podiceps auritus			
Eared grebe	kill (not eaten)	British Columbia	Stacey and Baird 1989
Podiceps nigricollis			
Pacific loon	harassed	British Columbia	Morton 1990
Gavia pacifica			
White-winged scoter	seen feeding	British Columbia	Odlum 1948
Melanitta fusca			
Pigeon guillemot	chases, kill	British Columbia	Stacey *et al.* 1990; R. W. Baird, pers. commun.
Cepphus columba			
Common murre	chases	British Columbia	Stacey *et al.* 1990; R. W. Baird, pers. com.
Uria aalge			

*Seen feeding on longlined fish.

References:

Bain, D. 1990. Examining the validity of inferences drawn from photo-identification data, with special reference to studies of the killer whale (*Orcinus orca*) in British Columbia. Rep. Int. Whaling Commn. Special Issue 12:93-100.

Baird, R.W., and P.J. Stacey. 1987. Foraging behavior of transient killer whales. Cetus7(1):33.

Baird, R.W., and P.J. Stacey.1988. Foraging and feeding behavior of transient killer whales. Whalewatcher (J. Amer. Cet. Soc.) 22:11-14.

Balcomb, K.C., J.R. Boran, and S.L. Heimlich. 1982. Killer whales in Greater Puget Sound. Rep. Int. Whaling Commn. 32:681-﹍﹍5.

Barrett-Lennard, L. 1992. Echolocation in wild killer whales (*Orcinus orca*). *M.S.* Thesis, University of British Columbia, Vancouver, B.C. 74pp.

Berzin, A.A., and V.L. Vladimirov. 1982. A new species of killer whale from the Antarctic. Priroda No. 6:31.

Bigg, M.A. 1982. An assessment of killer whale (*Orcinus orca*) stocks off Vancouver Island, British Columbia. Rep. Int. Whaling Commn. 32:655-666.

Bigg, M.A., G.E. Ellis, J.K.B. Ford, and K.C. Balcomb. 1987. Killer Whales: A study of their Identification, Genealogy, and Natural History in British Columbia and Washington State. Phantom Press, Nanaimo, B.C. 79pp.

Bigg, M.A., P.F. Olesiuk, G.M. Ellis, J.K.B. Ford, and K.C. Balcomb. 1990. Social organization and genealogy of resident killer whales (*Orcinus orca*) in coastal waters of British Columbia and Washington State. Rep. Int. Whaling Commn. Special Issue 12:383-405.

Bigg, M.A. and A. A. Wolman. 1975. Live-capture killer whale (*Orcinus orca*) fishery, British Columbia and Washington, 1962-73. J. Fish. Res. Board Can. 32:1213-1221.

Calambokidis, J., K. M. Langelier, P. J. Stacey, and R. W. Baird. 1990. Environmental contaminants in killer whales from Washington, British Columbia, and Alaska. Page 4 in Third International Orca Symposium, Victoria, B.C. Whale Museum, Friday Harbor, Wash. (Abstr.)

Dalheim, M.E. 1981. A review of the biology and exploitation of the killer whale, *Orcinus orca*, with comments on recent sightings from Antarctica. Rep. Int Whaling Commn. 31:541-546.

Diamond, J. 1992. The Third Chimpanzee. Harper Collins Publishers Inc. New York, N.Y.

Felleman, F.L., J.R. Heimlich-Boran, and R. Osborne. 1991. The feeding ecology of killer whales (*Orcinus orca*) in the Pacific Northwest. pp. 113-148. *In*: K. Pryor and K. S. Norris, eds. Dolphin Societies. Univ. of California Press. Berkeley, CA.

Ford, J.K.B. 1991. Vocal traditions among resident killer whales (*Orcinus orca*) in coastal waters of British Columbia. Can. J. Zool. 69:1454-1483.

Ford, J.K.B, and H.D. Fisher. 1982. Killer whale (*Orcinus orca*) dialects as an indicator of stocks in British Columbia. Rep. Int. Whaling Commn. 32: 671-679.

Ford, J.K.B., and D. Ford. 1981. The killer whales of B.C. Waters 5(1):1-32.

Gaskin, D.E. 1982. The ecology of whales and dolphins. Heinemann Educational Books, Inc. Portsmouth, N.H. 459pp.

Geraci, J.R., and D.J. St. Aubin. 1990. Sea mammals and oil: confronting the risks. Academic Press, Inc. New York, N.Y. 282pp.

Heise, K., G. Ellis, and C. Matkin. 1992. A catalogue of Prince William Sound killer whales, 1991. North Gulf Oceanic Society. Homer, AK. 51pp.

Hoezel, A.R. and G.A. Dover. 1991. Genetic differentiation between sympatric killer whale populations. Heredity 66:190-195.

Hoyt, E. 1981. Orca, the whale called killer. Camden House, Ontario, Canada. 287pp.

Leatherwood, S., K.C. Balcomb, C.O. Matkin, and G.E Ellis. 1984(b). Killer whales (*Orcinus orca*) of southern Alaska: results of field research 1984. Preliminary report. Hubbs Sea World Res. Inst. San Diego, CA. Tech. Rep. No. 84-175. 59pp.

Leatherwood, S., C.0. Matkin, J.D. Hall, and G.E. Ellis. 1990. Killer whales, *Orcinus orca*, photo-identified in Prince William Sound, Alaska, 1976 through 1987. Can. Field-Nat. 104(3):362-371.

Matkin, C.O. 1988. Status of Prince William Sound killer whales and the sablefish fishery in late 1987. Unpubl. rep. to Univ. of Alaska, Sea Grant Marine Adv. Program. Cordova, Alaska. 10pp.

Matkin, C.O. and E. Saulitis. 1994. Killer whale, *Orcinus orca*, Biology and Management in Alaska. U.S. Marine Mammal Commission. Washington, D.C.

Matkin, C.O., R. Steiner, and G.E. Ellis. 1987. Photoidentification and deterrent experiments applied to killer whales in Prince William Sound, Alaska, 1986. Univ. of Alaska, Sea Grant Marine Adv. Program. Cordova, Alaska. 16pp.

Matkin, C.O., G. M. Ellis, M.E. Dahleim, and J. Zeh. 1994. Status of killer whales in Prince William Sound, Alaska 1985-1992. *In* T.R. Loughlin ed., The Impact of the *Exxon Valdez* oil spill on marine mammals. Acad. Press. San Diego, CA. In press.

Morton, A.B. 1990. A quantitative comparison of the behavior of resident and transient forms of the killer whale off the central British Columbia coast. Rep. Int. Whaling Commn. Special Issue 12:245-248.

Myrick, A.C., Yochem, P.K., and Cornell, L.H. 1988. Toward calibrating dentinal layers in captive killer whales by use of tetracycline labels. Rit. Fiskideildar 11:285-296.

Obee, B. and G. Ellis. 1992. Guardians of the whales. Whitecap Books. Vancouver/ Toronto, Canada.

Olesiuk, P., M.A. Bigg, and G.M. Ellis. 1990. Life history and population dynamics of resident killer whales (*Orcinus orca*) in the coastal waters of British Columbia and Washington State. Rep. Int. Whaling Commn. Special Issue 12:209-243.

Saulitis, E.L. 1993. The vocalizations and behavior of the "AT" group of killer whales (*Orcinus orca*) in Prince William Sound, Alaska. M.S. Thesis, Univ. of Alaska, Fairbanks. 209pp.

Von Ziegesar, O., G. Ellis, C.O. Matkin, and B. Goodwin. 1986. Repeated sightings of identifiable killer whales (*Orcinus orca*) in Prince William Sound, Alaska, 1977- 1983. Cetus 6(2):9-13.

Von Ziegesar, O. ed. 1992. A catalogue of Prince William Sound humpback whales identified by fluke photographs between the years 1977 and 1991. North Gulf Oceanic Society. Homer, Ak. 42pp.

Index

Non-intrusive research 11
(see also acoustic monitoring and photoidentifica-
tion)
Norris, Kenneth 45, 62

Oceanaria 31, 72
Oil spill 34, 79, 81-84, 86-
89, 92

Photoidentification 1, 83
Play 62, 64
Pods 3, 18, 32, 33; aggre-
gations of 37, 63; defini-
tion of 20; dialects 45,
46-47; see also AB, Ad,
AE, AF, AG, AI, AJ, AK,
AN10, AN20, AX
Population studies 70-71
Prey species 95-98.

Radio transmitters 94
Range 20
Resting 57-58, 92
"Resident" killer whales 9,
16, 17, 18, 19, 20, 44, 45,
54; aggregations of 21;
avoid transients 23
Robbing longlines 76-78
Rubbing beaches 64

Salmon 1, 3, 6, 10, 59-60,
73, 80, 91, 97
Saulitis, Eva viii, 16, 21,
41, 46
Sea Grant Marine Advi-
sory Program 75
Sea otters 60, 97
Sea World 70-71, 78
Sexual activity 63-64
Social structure 20, 86

Sound 42
Spyhopping 62
Steiner, Rick 75ff.
Steller sea lions 53-54, 60,
96
Surface behavior 61-64

Tagging 10
Teeth 31
"Transient" killer whales
16, 17, 18, 2, 21, 48, 53-
54, 60, 62, 64, 66-67,
68; avoid residents 23;
ranges 23
Traveling 3, 19, 26, 55-56

Visibility 42
Vision 62
Vocalizations 42

Ziegesar, Olga viii, 71

Join with the Whale Researchers

Support the **NORTH GULF OCEANIC SOCIETY** and
LONG TERM WHALE RESEARCH in Prince William Sound!

Without private support our program could not go on. We ask you to join our effort. Your dollar will go directly into research and education. For a tax deductible donation of $25.00 or more you will receive an 8x10 black and white reproduction of a breaching transient killer whale (see page 14) and our annual newsletter. Donors of $100.00 or more also will receive a video of Prince William Sound's whales.

Please send this form with your donation to:
North Gulf Oceanic Society
P.O. Box 15244
Homer, Alaska 99603

Name: _____

Address: _____

I am interested in an adopt a whale program for:
killer whales_____ or humpback whales_____ (Please check)

I am 18 or over and am interested in whale research training programs ___

I would like a complete catalogue of Prince William Sound killer whales:
___ copies @ $12 postpaid.   I enclose _____

I would like a complete catalogue of Prince William Sound humpback whales: ___ copies @ $9 postpaid.   I enclose _____

Thank you for your support!